With thanks from
all the authors
for allowing us
to use your
material.

Carla

WORKING WITH HIGH-CONFLICT FAMILIES OF DIVORCE

WORKING WITH HIGH-CONFLICT FAMILIES OF DIVORCE

A GUIDE FOR PROFESSIONALS

Mitchell A. Baris, Ph.D.
Christine A. Coates, M. Ed., J.D.
Betsy B. Duvall, M.S.W.
Carla B. Garrity, Ph.D.
Elaine T. Johnson, J.D.
E. Robert LaCrosse, Ph.D.

JASON ARONSON INC.
Northvale, New Jersey
London

Production Editor: Elaine Lindenblatt

This book was set in 11 pt. New Baskerville by Alabama Book Composition of Deatsville, AL and printed and bound by Book-mart Press, Inc. of North Bergen, NJ.

Library of Congress Cataloging-in-Publication Data

Working with high-conflict families of divorce : a guide for professionals / Mitchell A. Baris . . . [et al.].
      p.   cm.
   Includes bibliographical references and index.
   ISBN 0-7657-0292-4
   1. Divorced parents—United States—Psychology.   2. Divorced parents—Counseling of—United States.   3. Parenting, Part-time—United States.
   4. Children of divorced parents—United States.   I. Baris, Mitchell A.
HQ834. W73   2000
306.89—dc21   00-038962

Printed in the United States of America on acid-free paper. For information and catalog write to Jason Aronson Inc., 230 Livingston Street, Northvale, NJ 07647-1731. Or visit our website: http://www.aronson.com

To all the children who have first-hand experience
with high-conflict divorce.

They are the reason we do this work.

Contents

PART III: THE HIGH-CONFLICT MODEL IN USE

PART IV: CASE-MANAGEMENT GUIDELINES

Preface

About fifteen years ago, the use of custody evaluations became widespread. These evaluations had existed before but were rare. Suddenly the courts viewed them as a tool for answers to the perplexing questions that judges had to address before making decisions. Basing judgments on issues such as degree of attachment, ability to foster a loving relationship with the nonresidential parent, and psychological aptness for parenthood, as defined by a mental health professional, seemed a good database for many of the questions for which judges had struggled to find answers. There was a honeymoon period when custody evaluations "flew high." After a time, attorneys viewed custody evaluations as helpful if they recommended what the attorneys' clients wanted, but something to be overcome if their clients did not like the outcome. A second evaluation was often the solution and, if the evaluators disagreed in their recommendations, the evaluations tended to cancel each other and then the decision was up to the judge as he reacted to good lawyering. Soon, custody evaluations were seen as only one piece of equipment in the attorney's armamentarium and not the special set of insights they once were considered. At times, evaluators, when they feared that parent alienation was a strong possibility, would recommend joint custody to prevent the target parent from being legally squeezed out. Sometimes evaluators made mistakes in their judgments because they were unable to determine whether the parental conflict was a temporary response to the divorce or a lasting uproar based on deep-seated emotional problems or entrenched conflict.

With high-conflict parents, thousands of dollars might be spent going back to court many times a year to fight over what—to the outsider—seemed to be highly inconsequential topics, such as whether the transfer of children between households should occur at a police station or a church. Sometimes, intense quarrels would arise when the children were exchanged, causing police intervention and the issuance of no-contact orders. Not that this kind of behavior did not exist between parents twenty-five years ago—but for those parents who could not stop fighting, a system had now come to be in which they could argue ad infinitum. With the advent of custody evaluations, quarrels were much more open to public scrutiny. Some courts and evaluators provided services and got to know these families well. Usually these couples did not have a well-constructed co-parenting plan, so such things as the definition of the Christmas holiday would have to be reinvented each year. The divorce settlement often included a "reasonable and liberal" visitation clause but with no specific guidelines. Even worse, the couple might have joint custody but one parent would have the tie-breaking vote if there was an impasse (i.e., sole custody masqueraded as joint). If angered, one parent might deny access to the other by saying at the door, "Johnny has a fever and can't go with you" or "Jean has a birthday party I forgot to tell you about so she can't go this weekend because it's on Saturday night." Everyone who reads this book will probably have their own war story about a flagrant bit of acting out between parents in an attempt to deny one or the other access to or the love of the children. Fortunately, most divorced parents do permit the other parent to continue being a parent. Those who do not make up a small, but enormously time-consuming, group.

A few monitoring and exchange services arose about twenty years ago in Denver. (The Children's Visitation Program, one of the first in the country, started in 1978.) These were organizations or professionals who offered to supervise transfers or, in the most dire of cases, offered supervised visitation services for children not thought to be safe if left alone with the nonresidential parent. From this came requests for more services, particularly for people the courts were simply tired of seeing. Litigation was used for quarrels over issues of minor concern to the court but of intense personal interest to the parents. Particularly characteristic of these high-conflict clients was their highly combative stance; their tendency to sabotage the best efforts of the court; and their tendency to exasperate their attorneys, mediators, and mental health professionals because "it was always something." This book arose out of demands for high-conflict post-divorce services, which had yet to be "invented."

In 1992 we were part of a group of Denver-metro lawyers and mental health professionals who met for mutual support as we worked with high-conflict couples. The group had nine members: Mitch Baris (psychologist), Christie Coates (attorney), Betsy Barbour Duvall (social worker), Carla Garrity (child psychologist), Bob Hovenden (social worker), Elaine Johnson (attorney), Marlene Knapp (social worker), Bob LaCrosse (child psychologist), and Arnie Swartz (social worker). We called ourselves the "high-conflict study group" and met monthly to develop a model of parenting coordination and consult regarding our more difficult cases. Our talk soon evolved into our trying to come up with the model we described as "parenting coordination."

After we had sketched out a model, we decided to take on a few cases at a reduced fee—because we felt we were still very much learning—and to use the whole group as a supervisor as we worked with our introductory cases. As one member put it, we used a Piagetian approach and learned most from our mistakes . . . and mistakes were myriad. Particularly troublesome were those that led our clients to fight us and sometimes flee. Flight always meant going back into court to battle things out. It was with these cases that we learned how important it was to forge an alliance with all of the attorneys involved in the case and not to directly attack a client's defenses.

We gave a few seminars to our local peers about what we were discovering and working on, and we met with a very positive reception. Garrity and Baris were in the throes of writing their second book, *Caught in the Middle* (1994), and were particularly interested in hearing about what other people were experiencing and in sharing their own experiences. Their book was published in 1994 and was well received.

Inquiries came pouring in. Parenting coordination became a buzz word, but one that had no real definition. Our sense was that many people began to jump aboard the parent-coordination "ship" without much of an idea of what they were getting into, and many had no mediation training nor sound intellectual familiarity with its concepts. While it seemed a great way to make money in a tightening market under managed care, many were, understandably, making the same naive mistakes we once did (and occasionally continue to do).

From the larger group of nine, six of us (Baris, Coates, Duvall, Garrity, Johnson, and LaCrosse—the names are ordered alphabetically, not by effort or contribution) spun off to write this book. The goal of the book is to present our definition of parenting coordination in a mediation-arbitration model. We met as a group about every six weeks, with pauses to write. For most of us it was difficult to get going, but once prose was on paper, we became excited about our progress. At times there were great similarities between our former peer-supervision group meetings and our current writing-group meetings. Writing a book by committee was a new experience for us. We have tried not to issue a book like the old political cartoon in which a bill is pictured leaving a Congressional committee room with the head of a lion, the neck of a giraffe, the body of an elephant, and the legs and feet of a horse, but we can assure the reader that everything in the book is come by with hard experience.

We present here a model of parenting coordination as it exists today. The model made a great deal of sense to us as we lived it, examined it, and adjusted our professional behaviors to it and the data it generated. As with any model, it is constantly evolving, and we feel we continue to grow and change as we become more experienced. What you are about to read presents the reasoned expression of our thinking and hands-on experience. We hope you will learn from our experience, profit from our mistakes as we have, and continue to improve the model of parenting coordination on your own.

Part I

Understanding High Conflict

High-conflict management—the phrase so easily said, the task so difficult to do. Whether you call yourself a Special Master, a Guardian *ad litem* (GAL), a Special Advocate, a Representative for the Child, or a Parenting Coordinator, work with high-conflict post-divorce couples (or high-conflict, never-married, now-separated parents) requires a special type of knowledge, a special type of personal stamina, and a special type of conceptualization of the dynamics and the issues. This book attempts to define the dynamics of high conflict and to identify the professional skills necessary to be of assistance. It also asks you to define exactly what kind of services you will be providing, and offers sample contracts and protocols to help get you started. It is based on the authors' experience in dealing with high-conflict couples and talks with others in the field.

There have been many changes in America's concepts of divorce. We have been gradually evolving a system that focuses on the needs of children as separate and distinct individuals with needs that must be addressed in the context of adult needs. We have come a long way from the concept of women and children as property.

CHILDREN AND THE LAW: HISTORICAL PERSPECTIVE

The law, as it relates to custody, has been continuously changing as shifting social mores thrust more families into the courtroom. Unfortunately, for the children involved, the legal system incorporates change very slowly. Although, in a broad sense, this pace serves to protect constitutional rights and personal freedom, it has not proven adequate in responding to the needs of children. In particular, the legal system has been slow to react to and incorporate the significant research conducted in the last two decades on child development and the impact of conflict and divorce upon children.

A history of divorce law demonstrates tremendous diversity in terms of how and when government has chosen to intercede into the dissolution of a marriage. Family matters, particularly relating to children, have traditionally been handled within the extended family and by the church. A brief review of the legal system and divorce law tends to be a synopsis of how religious and social philosophies are integrated with governmental intervention into families.

Historically, there are some, but very few, examples of a flexible attitude about divorce. At the time of Christ, "Roman marriage had become a private partnership of the most intimate nature, in which the parties were equal and shared in all rights. As marriage was founded on affection and consent, the parties had the right to dissolve it . . . and no judicial or other inquiry into the causes of the divorce was necessary" (Kitchen 1992, p. 5). This perspective, which included equal rights between genders, is rarely seen in a historical analysis of marriage and divorce.

The rise of Christianity set forth an edict that divorce was wrong, ". . . he who made them from the beginning made them male and female, and said, 'For this reason a man shall leave his father and mother and be joined to his wife, and the two shall become one' . . . What therefore God has joined together, let not man put asunder . . ." (Bible, Matthew 19:3–9). This theme of marital indissolubility became a fundamental basis of English law, which, in turn, provided a basis for the legal doctrines of the early American colonies.

During the colonial period, divorce was deemed a civil matter and was no longer the providence of church officials.

However, there remained a very rigid moral component, and punishment of one party was an inherent result. The first recorded decree of divorce in the Massachusetts Bay Colony, in 1636, provided,

> James Luxford, being presented for having two wives, his last marriage was declared void, or a nullity thereof, and to be divorced, not to come to the sight of her whom he last took, and he to be sent away for England by the first opportunity: and all that he hath is appointed to her whom he last married, for her and her children; he is also fined 100 pounds, and to be set in the stocks an hour upon a market day after the lecture (Massachusetts Colony Records 1639, vol. 1, p. 283, cited in Cowley 1890, p. 16). [Halem 1980, pp. 14–15]

The colonial period in the United States embraced an economic base that favored a view of children as property. As is often the case in agricultural societies, children were essentially workers who could favorably impact the economic success of a family. "[T]he economic needs of the colonies determined the custodial arrangements of children, superseding child nurturing and often biological parenthood. Childhood . . . was a time of work, and for preparation to become adult workers" (Mason 1994, p. 46). During this period, the emphasis on the role of children as they related to the workforce favored fathers in custody determinations.

During the early nineteenth century, the grounds for divorce expanded. The economic base of the country was shifting to one of urban industrialization, and the role of children in a family undertook a transformation due, at least in part, to a declining birthrate. Between 1800 and 1900, the average birthrate for a white woman dropped from 7.04 to 3.56 (Mason 1994, p. 51). The emphasis on children as field workers diminished, and the role of mothers in the family increased as fathers left the home to work elsewhere. This shifting of societal views of both mothers and children was reflected in divorce cases, which, although presumptively still awarding the father custody, began to look more closely at the father. In fact, toward the end of this time period, the custody of children was beginning to be awarded to the mother when the father's behavior was clearly contrary to social norms. "If the father is shown unfit, he may be deprived of the custody of his child, and the court will appoint a guardian *or* transfer it to the mother" (13 Johns., 418, cited in Chadman 1899, emphasis added).

During the early twentieth century, there was tremendous variance in the bases of custody awards. Different courts, even within the same state, used extremely diverse standards to award custody. In some courts, fathers continued to have priority and, in other courts, the "tender years doctrine" began to be implemented. This concept, focusing on the bond between mother and child, shifted the presumption, particularly for young children, from fathers to mothers.

In 1925, the Honorable Judge Benjamin Cardozo first introduced the concept of "best for the interests of the child" as a means of determining custody. The concept of "best interests," although defined differently over time and in different jurisdictions, continues to be the dominant criterion in determining today's custody decisions.

The mid-nineteenth century saw the end of the presumption that fathers received custody. The government viewed its role as one of protecting and promoting children (Mason 1994, p. 119). The tender years doctrine continued to be favored, and fathers were viewed not as an appropriate custodian but, rather, as an economic resource for the child. In many jurisdictions, this philosophy continues today.

The later half of the twentieth century has seen a dramatic shift in divorce law. The law, as it should, has been changing in response to the transformations taking place in American life. The concept of no-fault divorce, the mobile nature of our population, increasing economic independence of women, gender equality, research on child development, and the impact of divorce on children have all had significant roles in custody determinations.

In the past decade, perhaps the most significant impact on custody cases has been the increasing roles that professionals, other than attorneys and judges, play in custody cases. The "expert" whose duty is to advise the court on a child's best interests has had an immense impact on how custody decisions are made. Custody evaluators, social workers, psychologists, psychiatrists, and Guardians *ad litem* were initially viewed as a panacea for the court in custody determinations.

Unfortunately, the reality is that there has been no panacea for the children who are the subjects of custody cases. Many parents, regardless of the efforts made by countless experts during a case, remain in high conflict. These cases continue to clog already-crowded courtroom dockets with post-trial motions and modifications. They cause immeasurable pain to the families and endless frustration to the various professionals involved.

The legal system now faces challenges unlike those in the past. The tension between protecting individual rights and freedom from intrusion by the state and protecting children and families from the harm created by divorce taxes the most sophisticated and progressive of systems.

The challenge of today's divorce law is to utilize and incorporate the psychological and sociological research in a manner that helps families in high conflict but yet preserves the sanctity of the family from unnecessary intrusion by the government. To achieve the proper balance, an alliance between the legal and mental health professions is essential. It is within this underlying framework that the concept of parenting coordination has been successfully implemented.

The research on divorce and its impact on families remains in its infancy. The far-reaching effects of divorce on our society are only beginning to be seen, and the impact on a generation of children is just beginning to be understood. It is a fact, however, that children in a high-conflict divorce are at risk of serious damage. This damage may never be repaired, and these children, as parents, perpetuate future generations who are adversely impacted. As a society, we cannot afford children who are caught in the middle of conflict, unable to develop properly, become good parents, and be productive members of society.

Our legal system was designed to protect individual freedom and liberty. It was never intended to resolve the psychological and social problems created by families who can't stay together or live peacefully apart. The legal system is, however, the social structure in which intervention with these families must take place.

The model of parenting coordination set forth in this book is intended to integrate into existing legal structures. It is essential that a Parenting Coordinator be familiar with the law in his/her particular jurisdiction and that the role of a Parenting Coordinator be structured in a manner that is appropriate based upon the legal and ethical standards in that jurisdiction.

protection of a court order to ultimately decide issues the parents cannot. The court maintains oversight and can review any decision made by these high-conflict managers, but the breaking of a parental impasse first falls to these individuals. In this book we refer to a high-conflict manager as a Parenting Coordinator (PC). We use it as a generic or umbrella term. By Parenting Coordinator, we mean an individual assigned by the court or by stipulation through the court whose task is to educate, mediate, and perhaps arbitrate parental disputes over the raising of their children. We are aware that some areas use the term "Parenting Coordinator" as a real label for an individual providing these services. We have deliberately broadened the definition of Parenting Coordinator to include all those individuals who work to help parents in high conflict resolve their impasses so life can move on and their children can be reasonably free from stress and anxiety.

Regardless of one's title and regardless of one's formal training, someone working as a high-conflict dispute manager must have a blend of professional skills that go beyond simply being a professionally trained mediator, psychotherapist, or attorney. Although training in one of these professions is helpful and can provide a good foundation upon which to build the veritable salad of skills required to be a PC, no single discipline's training provides all the skills needed. In our experience, during the course of work with a high-conflict couple, a PC may be called upon to provide or effect a number of services. For instance, early in a PC's work with a couple, he or she might wish to do a psychological evaluation so as to understand an individual's perception of reality. The PC might do an analysis of the extended family dynamics if such family members play influential roles in either creating or soothing conflict. The PC will undoubtedly provide child development information as to, for instance, the world-view and needs of a typical three-year-old. He or she will probably offer examples of how other families have solved the same problem that the conflicted parents cannot seem to resolve. The PC may have to mediate a dispute by helping people understand what lies behind their rigid positions and pointing out the commonalties that lie unseen amidst the conflict. The PC might arbitrate and certainly will need to know the legal requirements in conducting a valid arbitration process. He or she will often be interviewing teachers and therapists as to how they see the children. In particular, the PC may serve as a coordinator of services to the family so that the helpers do not start "bumping into each other" in terms of the advice they give or where they lead their client. It is a truism that a therapist forms an alliance with his or her client and normally sees the world through the client's eyes. In a high-conflict situation, therapist myopia can be harmful because often their client will vilify the other parent and draw the therapist into their version of the truth as the only version of the truth. So, although a professional may start out with a good foundation in his or her discipline, many skills must be added to the repertoire to handle the multifaceted requirements of parent coordination. This book lays out the range of skills needed.

Of course, one cannot be all things to all people. "A jack-of-all-trades and a master of none" is *not* an acceptable description of a high-conflict manager. To know which skills you have mastered and to be able to clearly state what you can then offer as services is the sign of a true professional. Venturing where you are not qualified is dangerous to both you and the client. There is no harm in not being able to do some things. Harm comes from being drawn into areas beyond your skill level and behaving "as if" you were an expert. The seductive pull from clients is particularly strong, especially at the beginning of the working relationship because you will be seen as "the savior."

If there is one unifying trait that cuts across all high-conflict couples, it is a breathtaking inability to self-observe. By this is meant an inability to step back and try to view oneself as others might see you. Here is an example one author recently experienced with a high-conflict couple. The couple have two children, a boy age 7 and a girl age 12. The mother fears the father will do great harm to her children. She is a "by the numbers" hover mother whereas the father is very laid back, a poet, a recovering hippie, and loath to take orders. The children have a strong alliance with their mother. They are not victims of parent alienation as much as they are strongly convinced their mother needs them to make her life work. When the children visit father, mother calls daily. When this was stopped by the PC, the eldest child would sneak out to a pay phone to call. In their alliance with mother, to prove their love, the children would tell mother those things that fed into her view that father was an accident waiting to happen and that her children would be hurt. The children broke into a case where the father kept BB guns, went into the backyard to shoot at squirrels, and called their mother on the cell phone to tell her what they were doing while father was away at the store. Mother called the police. The father found their arrival deeply humiliating. One child found a bag of "green stuff" while searching through father's bureau drawers. Mother suggested the next time he went he take a baggie, which she supplied, and remove some of the "green stuff." She had it analyzed by a lab and sure enough it was marijuana. She called the police who refused to pursue the issue. Mother then went on a vacation with her children to a local lake. Much to her horror, as she was walking down the small main street of the tourist town, father popped out of a bar, called his children to him and introduced them to some of his friends. Later the same day, he appeared at a distance when they were at the beach and called to them and waved hello. Mother, in a panic, called the PC and voiced her fears of what father might do. "Why is he here? What does he want? He is almost stalking us!" Mother parked her car away from the rental cabin and told the front desk at the resort to tell no one where she and her children were staying. What was very clear to the PC and to the Guardian *ad litem* (GAL) on the case was that father was trying to re-create for mother the terrible sense of intrusiveness and lack of peace he felt when mother intruded on his time with his children. It was a "See, now you can know how it feels!" statement on his part. She simply did not get it because she had no empathy for what he experienced from her.

As a PC, you will be confronted again and again by people who simply cannot assume any perspective but their own. In adults, this is a major way of learning about and understanding interpersonal relationships, so the PC is confronted with great challenges in trying to get his or her point across so the client can use alternate strategies. We speak to this in Chapter 2.

We consider the main goal of parenting coordination to be to protect children from harm. Research indicates in divorce, or in intact but high-conflict families, the greatest damage to children occurs when the children are subjected to conflict, particularly when they are used as a medium through which the conflict takes place. Here we speak of putting children in the middle. A parent places a child in the middle when the child is asked to be a carrier of adult messages, asked to keep secrets, or asked to serve as a spy in the other household (as in our example above). When a parent trashes the other parent to the child, half of that child is being trashed also. Such issues take their toll on a child's self-esteem and sense of well-being. Any movement along the continuum from conflict to cooperation, no matter how small, is a move to benefit the child. That is the bottom line for a PC.

In the following chapters we hope to introduce you to a user-friendly guidebook for high-conflict management. It is not intended as a cookbook, that is, "Do this and you will be wildly successful." Rather, it is a distillation of experience from a field that is still in its infancy. Our assumption is that if you have the principles of high-conflict management to guide you, you can invent your own behavior, carefully tailored to your particular task at hand. Independent functioning is our goal, not dependent. The materials included as well as the experiences discussed will provide you with the building blocks to transcend being just a member of a particular discipline to being an informed practitioner who rises above the simple boundaries of your discipline. When working with high conflict, it is as important to know what you don't know as what you do know. Herein is presented the scope of what you need to know, even if it means having to say, "I don't provide that kind of service."

2

The Dynamics of High Conflict

Most couples are in conflict at the time of separation and throughout the period of financial settlements and parenting arrangements. This period of turmoil typically lasts from one to two years. Gradually, most divorcing couples pick up the pieces of their shattered dreams, resolve their anger and bitterness, and go on with their lives in a reasonable manner. Some, however, never recover. They remain locked in entrenched and serious conflict endlessly.

What do these parents fight about?

1. Profound mistrust of their ex-spouse's parenting skills, which frequently includes allegations and accusations of abuse, mistreatment, and poor judgment.
2. Parenting time and access to the children.
3. Behavioral problems the children are displaying and who is to blame.
4. Being disparaged by the other parent to the point of

being convinced the children are being "poisoned" or "brainwashed."

These fights play out in court, in public, and in front of the children. They involve bitter words, malicious threats, and, at times, explosive violence or, in some cases, icy silence, refusal to communicate, and messages sent through the children.

These parents forget or fail to care about the needs of the children in their intense desire for revenge, vengeance, and a desire to win at all costs. The psychological outcome for the children of these parents can be tragic. The children deserve better, but the legal remedies have not proved effective when the conflict is intense between the parents.

Understanding the dynamics of these high-conflict families is an essential stepping-stone to untangling the process, freeing the children from its toll, and offering them hope for a healthier and happier future. As common as divorce is today, and as frequently as parents believe it will bring greater personal happiness or relief, at best it still represents trauma and loss. Divorce evokes profound feelings of helplessness, humiliation, shame, and anger. For high-conflict couples, these feelings are greater than they have the capacity to manage and regulate. The flood of feelings assaults their sense of self and wounds them narcissistically to a profound extent. Fighting, taking control, and being in charge restores a false sense of equilibrium and power to these fragile and narcissistically wounded individuals.

One high-conflict couple continually involved their twin boys, age 11, directly in their conflict with one another. After working with the parents, the Parenting Coordinator (PC) felt it important to see the children in order to gain some sense of what these children, about whom the parents argued and fought so passionately, were really like. The children were seen for a single session. One of the boys seemed particularly tense. Unlike most children who keep a distance between themselves and the PC, particularly during the first meeting, this child pulled up a footstool so he was sitting about eighteen inches from the shoulder of the PC.

The interview went well. The children had a "chatty" quality to their voices when they talked about their father, as if spouting a parental line. The next day the mother (who had brought the children) left the following message on the PC's voice mail: "I need to talk with you. I have been reviewing the tape and I think you were unfair in some of the questions you were asking my boys." After hearing the message, the PC thought, "I don't remember taping the session. Did I tape the session? If I taped the session, how did she get a copy of the tapes? I don't recall handing any out." The reaction was one of initial confusion based on a simple, erroneous assumption that reasonable human behavior was shared by the mother and her sense of how people treated one another. It was with a rising sense of rage that the PC realized that one of the children had been "wired" with a hidden tape recorder without the PC's knowledge, and that the session with the children was not confidential as the PC had stated to them. The children knew it was not confidential while the PC did not; a very important interpersonal boundary had been pierced. The PC's initial rage response, fortunately experienced only individually and with selected other colleagues, was a reaction to a profound sense of boundary invasion. The PC had been "had" without a glimmer of recognition.

The PC had a sudden surge of empathy for why the boys were so aligned with their mother. The intrusive assaultiveness of the incident demonstrated how impossible it would be to live un-aligned in mother's highly aligned world. It was thus much easier for the PC to be empathic with the boys than it was to be empathic with the mother. The PC learned more from being the target of her narcissistically distorted behavior than from standing on the sidelines and watching what was happening to the boys.

The mother in the above example felt beleaguered by her ex-husband's constant badgering that she was a bad mother and an evil person. She felt the father kept making claims that were untrue and that, in particular, professionals involved in the children's lives kept distorting what she or the children said. The tape recording of the session was her desperate effort to have concrete evidence that she could play back to the professional who denied ever having said any such thing or denied that her children had taken a particular stance. She felt massively assaulted by what she considered to be the father's lies and the professionals' distortions. Her sons had reached the point of strong alignment with mother. This was a protective stance because the parents' attitudes were so polarized the twins could not remain neutral and feel safe. Each parent demanded, through thorough trashing of the other parent, that the children take sides. Theirs was a "take no prisoners" battle. The boy who sat next to the PC and who was "wired" showed great distress on his face, so one assumes that he was aware, at some level, that the PC might not approve. He was not as blinded as his mother. There was never an opportunity to follow up with the children in this case. Shortly after this incident, the mother released tapes of the children's conversations with their father, who had crudely savaged the mother to the boys on a dinner visit when she had them wired. When the father heard "his" tapes, he totally withdrew and allowed the mother's new husband to adopt the boys. He has not seen them since.

The most telling sign of narcissism in the above tale is the mother's comment, "I have been reviewing the tape. . . ." Nowhere does she introduce the concept that she needed to inform the PC that she had taped the session. She merely started from the center of her universe and began the conversation. This is an example of extreme narcissistic entitlement and narcissistic self-absorption, qualities that usually define a high-conflict situation. The PC was an "object" upon whom the mother was acting; any professional or personal expectations about the niceties of social interaction were irrelevant to the mother's agenda. The PC was acted *upon*, not interacted *with*. Such transactions are common with at least one partner of a high-conflict couple. The question then is how does a parent become so self-absorbed and so narcissistically preoccupied as to be able to act out with the serenity of "knowing" he or she is right.

NARCISSISM

Narcissism can be defined as a normal or abnormal regulation of self-esteem. Regulation is the key word in the definition. In other words, any mental activity dedicated to maintaining the structure and stability of the self is narcissistic. As Stolorow and Lachman (1980) note:

> Narcissism embodies those mental operations whose *function* is to regulate self-esteem . . . and to maintain the cohesion and stability of the self representation. . . . The relation of narcissism to self-esteem is analogous to the relation between a thermostat and room temperature. A thermostat is not equivalent to room temperature, nor is it the only determinant of room temperature. It is the function of a thermostat to regulate and stabilize room temperature in the face of a multitude of forces which threaten to raise or lower it. . . . When self-esteem is threatened, significantly lowered, or destroyed, then narcissistic activities are called into play in an effort to protect, restore, repair and stabilize it. [p. 20ff.]

Narcissism is a set of psychological functions that are called into play when an individual's self-esteem is assaulted. Narcissistic coping activities serve to bring the sense of damage back to a manageable level. Essentially this is psychological repair work so an individual can restore self-esteem or a cohesive sense of self. Depending on the depth of the wound to self-esteem, narcissistic activities are modest or intense, and the outcome or final adjustment to regain equilibrium can be considered as normal or abnormal.

Narcissistic "rebalancing" of self-esteem becomes maladaptive to the degree that a person must distort reality to regain a sense of equilibrium. For instance, the more difficult it is for someone to accept the fact that he or she did something wrong, the more likely that person is to feel blameless and to project the blame onto an event or someone else. A mild example would be a person who blames a store for not stocking dress shirts properly when he gets home and finds that he bought the wrong size. Here the issue is whether the store should have stocked properly or the person should have read the label before he bought. If making a dumb mistake is a bit too threatening for a person's self-image and self-esteem, then someone else must be blamed.

The dictionary definition of self-esteem is "the regard one has for the dignity of one's character." Dignity refers to one's sense of self-worth. Self-esteem is essentially the sense of worthwhileness, or one's value as a human being. Narcissism is not self-esteem or self-love per se, but the actions a person engages in to be able to hold oneself in high regard. Narcissism is a process in human functioning that enables an individual to monitor and adjust self-perception as a worthy individual. It functions across the continuum of human adjustment.

Self-esteem normally fluctuates according to the gratifying or frustrating experiences an individual has with others, as well as weighing actual performance against personal ideals or standards. The closer actual performance is to one's self-image, the more contentment is felt and the more feelings of being competent and worthy, and the less threat there is to self-esteem. Self-esteem is vulnerable to assaults by personal standards and by those set in childhood.

Everyone has experienced assaults on their self-esteem. Most well-functioning people can quickly conjure up, if asked, some assault on their self-esteem that, perhaps even years later, still creates a "psychic twinge" as they think about the incident. For instance, one of our colleagues in his youth functioned during the summer as a live-in child-care provider to three children of a well-to-do medical professional on the East Coast. The summer was spent in idyllic surroundings at a beach on the Atlantic. The entire family had gone to the yacht club for a Sunday dinner. Our colleague excused himself to go to the bathroom. Upon his return, one of his little charges leaned over and whispered that his fly was open. It was surreptitiously zipped under the table. At the end of the meal, when he rose to leave, a corner of the tablecloth that had caught in the zipper caused the tablecloth to be pulled. A glass fell and conversation stopped in the dining room while everyone stared in the direction of the sound. The scene seemed to be straight out of a Marx Brothers' comedy, but to the "victim" it was life's most embarrassing moment. It was experienced as if the entire world had stopped, looked, laughed (especially laughed), and committed the scene to memory to repeat at parties for the rest of their lives. But probably the only person with an *active* memory of the event some forty years later is the "victim." The incident dealt a strong narcissistic blow, particularly since, at age 17, being "cool" was among life's most important values and goals. The memory, however, has become a tale to be told to friends and joked about. While open about it now, the faint psychic twinge on the umpteenth retelling, however, still indicates that the narcissistic wound carries a slightly tender scab.

Narcissistic Wounds

Divorce can be a very humiliating experience, even for psychologically healthy people. Those who have fragile self-esteem are especially vulnerable to "falling apart" in reaction to the shame they feel when their marriages fail. One father who was quite a loner and struggling to advance in life was devastated by his wife's blatant affair during their marriage. He felt thoroughly humiliated and openly criticized his wife to everyone, including supermarket clerks. He began drinking again after many years of abstinence and, unfortunately, only further humiliated himself by his drunken actions. His abuse of alcohol can be seen as an attempt to numb the psychic pain and glue together the pieces of his shattered sense of self. Of course, it didn't work. The children witnessed violent rages against their mother and grandparents, were scared of their father, and didn't want to spend much time with him. After a custody dispute, he and his wife were awarded joint custody and the children went to live predominately with mom. The dad remained rageful and depressed and chose not to see his children at all, saying he was not in financial or emotional shape to be a father at that time. Although he was unable to recover from the humiliation of the divorce sufficiently to function as a dad, he at least recognized his incapacity. His plan was to work and try to recover; we hope he can.

When self-esteem is threatened, there is often a distortion of reality. During times of stress, such as a divorce, distortions of reality are common. Such distortions become problematic and perhaps a sign of a mental disorder only when they remain as distortions and are not modified, corrected, or eliminated by incoming additional information. For instance, a sleeping person suddenly awakened in the night by a sound in the house can get worked up into a veritable frenzy about the possibility of a burglar. Getting up, checking, finding nothing, and then falling back to sleep would be a normal response to feedback. A person who continued to be convinced, even with no evidence, that someone was nonetheless there, would be a person who could not utilize corrective feedback to modify the perception that the noise was an evil intruder. Carried to extreme, one would then begin to question such a person's reality testing.

Along with distortions of reality, hopefully transient and modifiable, can come a distortion of the perception of boundaries between people. In the initial case example in this chapter, the mother had a very distorted perception of where the boundaries lay among herself, her children, and the PC. Between two healthy people, boundaries are seen similarly, even if never verbalized. The world is full of *residual rules*—those rules that often are not formally taught but that everyone absorbs merely by being in the culture. The rules that you do not spit in the piano or blow your nose on your hostess's sleeve are "known" but rarely formally taught. We pick them up through "osmosis" by being raised in a common culture. A sense of boundaries can also exist between people of two very different levels, such as a parent and a child. If one thinks of boundaries as a set of concentric circles such as one would see in a halved onion, one can visualize each ring as a boundary, and as one gets closer to the center, or core, one steps over a boundary with increasing caution. A major task in developing a relationship with another human being is to recognize that boundaries exist and that there must be a way of crossing them or passing through them without destroying them. For instance, it is common for a parent to say to a small child, "I am cold, you put on a jacket." Here the parent does not recognize a boundary because the adult perceives the small child appropriately as having limited capability to plan ahead and anticipate the consequences of behavior or lack of behavior as the situation might warrant. Such a statement to an adolescent could trigger World War III because the adolescent will experience the statement as a severe boundary transgression—adolescents assume, without inquiry, that parent and child are equals. Such a request does not respect the boundary of individual differences, self-determination, and responsibility for one's self—all major adolescent preoccupations.

The normal process for crossing an interpersonal boundary is empathy. Empathy can be defined as the act of identifying with the feelings or thoughts of another person. In other words, the capacity to identify (in the sense of recognizing) with another person's thoughts or feelings, normally through a base of common, shared experiences, enables a closer and more intimate relationship. There are three requirements of the person empathizing: (1) identification with the other person (i.e., perceive similarities in experiences); (2) maintaining a clear sense of the boundary, even if there is a shared experience; and (3) employing the mutually shared experience to join with the other person in a way that is helpful to that individual. For instance, occasionally a therapist will experience a real sense of connection with a client. Often that sense of connection is because the therapist can identify or recognize highly similar background commonalties so communication can take place in an almost shorthand form. Typically, these are considered to be wonderful clients because there is a strong sense of connection and shared experience. If boundaries are not respected and observed, there may be an obliteration of two psychologically distinct people, only a sense of a unit of one. It is important to note that an empathizer must have a strong sense of self and personal boundaries so as to not slide over into a union in which "what I feel is what you feel." If not, one then is at a risk to move dangerously close to pathological symbiosis, in which it is difficult to tell where one's individuality and separateness stops and the other's starts. It is important to note that merging is normal and healthy when it occurs temporarily in early parent–child relationships and in adult intimate relationships.

A high-conflict couple will usually be comprised of at least one (perhaps both) individual who cannot empathize. A narcissistically wounded parent has difficulty defining an interpersonal boundary and finding a means to cross it. Typically such a parent distorts his/her perception of the other person. For instance, common in high-conflict divorce are charges of sexual, physical, or psychological abuse. It is wise to have enough information on each parent's background so as to know whether he or she was sexually, physically, or psychologically abused during childhood. If so, the groundwork has been laid for a possible blurring of boundaries. Abused parents can see their children as being harmed by their ex-spouse as they themselves were harmed as children. This represents, of course, identification without boundaries: "It happened to me, now it is happening to you because I experienced it as a child." It is also common for people who have been abused as children to marry people who are in fact abusive.

As noted earlier, there is either no reality check or, even with a reality check, the parent remains rigidly stuck in what is essentially a delusional system based on childhood experiences. Here, the child *within* the parent is seen as the same person as the parent's child. So, one pathological adaptation to the narcissistic wound of divorce is to draw a circle around oneself and one's child, see the two as identical, and experience any assault on either as an assault on both and any past history of assault or insult as a mutually shared experience.

Another pathological adjustment to a divorce-related narcissistic wound is to draw a hard, impermeable boundary around oneself and the child and to have no capacity to empathize with the other parent. This is a serious distortion because, of course, the parents have shared rearing the child and, one assumes, they share extensive common experiences. But such a nonempathic parent does not see the other parent as being a parent of the same child. The other parent is viewed as a stranger. Such sharp, rigid boundaries permit the wounded parent to treat the other in astoundingly cruel ways without a twinge of guilt.

When self-esteem is abnormally regulated and narcissistic pathology exists, the boundary between the individual and the ex-spouse is deeply distorted. The boundary is frequently drawn in a rigid, nonpenetrable way so that the narcissistically wounded person can be both emotionally and interpersonally detached. This results in the kind of relationship in which a person can appear cold and ruthless because there is no empathy for the other, who is seen as a "feelingless" object to be acted upon. An example of this is a case in which a very cold and aloof surgeon father insisted that his two latency-age children watch him dissect the family cat, who had just died, so he could demonstrate to them how the circulatory system worked. He was oblivious to the children's agony at watching their cat being cut apart and he was ultimately stunned by their hysterical reaction. The discrepancy between the father's perception of the cat as a tool for a lesson and the children's perception of the cat as a loved family pet was profound.

Narcissistically wounded parents who lack empathy free themselves for unfeeling assaults on the other parent by over-identifying with the children. Clinical signals of such a personality include the parent who refers to the other parent in the third person or by a formal title such as "Mr. Smith." One test is for the PC to ask the parent who is seen with the children a question about the family. Small children, in particular, will frequently include the absent parent in their conversation. But a parent who is lacking in empathy and overidentified with the children will often say, "No, we can't include her because she is not a member of our family." The same might be said about a family pet whose "custody" fell to the other household. The signal is that the parent is drawing a line for the children that the children would not normally create.

Another manifestation of a boundary issue is when an attack or a slight on the parent is also seen as an attack or slight on the children. This is a perceptual distortion of reality as the parent thinks that the children experience the divorce the same way the parent does. An example is a mother who insists that her 4-year-old cannot tolerate being with the father and the mother in the same room, when, in fact, it is the mother who cannot tolerate being in the same room with the father. It is her own tension, not the father per se, that makes the children tense.

People who do not experience grave difficulties with the maintenance of their self-image and self-esteem will reach out to another, a significant other, or a friend merely to sort out what has happened and reassure themselves, based on their own internal knowledge of themselves, that they are okay. Even if they have made an error, their attitude is one of analyzing the mistake, moaning about it perhaps, but learning from it and moving on. It does not become a central, structuring memory of the person's life. An example is the person who comes home from a hard day at the office, where little seemed to go right, talks with a spouse, sorts it out, and feels better. A signal that this is going on can be seen when the complainer feels irritated when the listener tries to offer solutions, and the response is, "No, no, I do not want you to tell me what to do, I just want you to listen to me!" However, people with narcissistic wounds who are having difficulty healing tend to use other listeners just to validate their own perceptions; they do not use the other person as a sounding board, they do not let their ideas in, they merely remain focused on their own complaints, irritations, etc. They, in essence, are rewriting history while drawing in their listener to join them on their side whether the listener indicates agreement or not.

Levels of Narcissistic Wounds

Johnston and Campbell (1988) describe three different levels of handling narcissistic wounds (see Table 2–1). The first level is the one described above, in which narcissistic individuals use other people to confirm their worthiness by merely listening and caring for them. Most people do this from time to time. This is the least worrisome level.

People with a second-level narcissistic wound require not only that they be listened to and comforted, but also that the listener *agree* with their opinion, that is, that the other parent is bad. A deeper level of affirming response is required by those with second-level wounds because they need not just support, but active support, for their perceptions. The listener is put into the position of needing to agree, for example, that the ex-spouse is "no good—Machiavellian," "sly," or whatever descriptors the wounded person is using.

The third and most pathological level is that in which the wounded individual needs support and agreement not only that his or her perception of the situation is correct, but, in addition, that the ex-spouse is so intentionally hurtful that revenge is

TABLE 2–1. TYPOLOGY OF NARCISSISTICALLY VULNERABLE DISPUTING PARENTS

Common Emotional Reactions to Divorce	Restitutive or Defensive Strategy	Behavioral Consequences Re: Custody/Access	Behavioral Consequences Re: Child (Meaning of Child)	Marital Partners and Interactions
Type A (N-72)				
Blow to self-esteem	Restore self-pride Raise self-esteem	Seek custody or decreased access to:	Child's preference for self over ex-spouse increases selfpride	A's married to A's (16 couples)
1. Low self-image Hurt Depression Feelings of failure, inadequacy, rejection	Rationalization Intellectualization Repression Sublimation	1. Show they are good, not failures, and not deserving rejection	Dependent on child's validation, recognition, and approval	Struggle to maintain respective self-esteem Escalating resistance to supporting the other until respected
2. Inflated self-image Shock Mild indignation Disappointment Feelings of disrespect and dis-acknowledgment		2. Gain acknowledgment, validation, approval, confirmation Refusal to cooperate until supported (Usually external forces lead to custody dispute)	Burdens child who has to reassure parent Concern over positive evaluation impedes relaxed and natural relationship with child, interferes with good parental judgment; parenting may become exaggerated to highlight "good" caretaking	

Type B (N-60)

	Get rid of badness, put badness onto spouse	Seek custody to:	Child is narcissistic extension, not separate from self, "feels as parent feels"	1. B's married to B's (18 couples)
Narcissistic wound or insult	Simple projection Projective identification Splitting Denial	Prove spouse is fundamentally bad, wrong: Show self as superior		Bitter, active disputes Each externalizes and projects blame
Pervasive or exaggerated sense of badness	Externalization Idealization/devaluation Exaggerated grandiosity	Court will judge: Judge is authority who will vindicate	Idealized view of child and relation with child: "badness" in child seen as fault of other	2. A's married to B's (20 couples)
Humiliation		Judge is idealized or devalued, depending on how s/he rules	Child is seen as judge who vindicates and as source of admiration; may need child to actively dislike other parent	Similar to A's married to C's, but A's have shown more passive resistance and B's showed less active aggressive threats (than C's)

29

TABLE 2–1. TYPOLOGY OF NARCISSISTICALLY VULNERABLE DISPUTING PARENTS (*continued*)

Common Emotional Reactions to Divorce	Restitutive or Defensive Strategy	Behavioral Consequences Re: Custody/Access	Behavioral Consequences Re: Child (Meaning of Child)	Marital Partners and Interactions
Type C (N-15)				
Narcissistic injury	Need to recoup losses, hurt back, or counterattack	Seek custody to:	Child involved indirectly to attempt to seek revenge	Almost all C's married to A's (14 of 15 couples)
Feelings of:		1. Counterattack, hurt, punish, retaliate, for revenge	Child used as weapon to punish ex: held to hurt spouse	Dependent, inadequate, and insecure A's were actively dominated and insulted by critical C parents
Exploitation	Projective-identification	2. Rescue child from demonic other	Try to enlist child in denigration or ex; pull for alliance which, if successful, supports view of self as "right"	Frightened and hurt, A's avoided and withdrew, failing to correct distortions of C parents
Injustice	Delusional projection	Judge viewed as ally or persecutor	Child as primitive ally, co-conspirator (if seen on self's side); child may be seen as persecutor and be rejected (if seen on ex's side)	
Humiliation	Reversal			
Being tricked	Acting out			

This table is adapted from training material developed by J. Johnston and L. E. G. Campbell and is reprinted here with permission. A full explication of this table is available in Johnston and Campbell's book *Impasses of Divorce: The Dynamics and Resolution of Family Conflict*, copyright © 1988 The Free Press.

justified. The defensive maneuver in this category is one in which the wounded individual projects his/her own anger onto the ex-spouse and thereby sees that anger as the ex's anger directed at him/her. Because it is cast as purposeful and deliberate, any means are, therefore, justified to counteract it.

One client, for instance, was enraged at his ex-wife because she made access to their son very difficult. Visits were canceled at the last minute because the boy was sick or had a birthday party to attend. In actuality, the mother *was* doing this, but her motivation was to protect the child, who complained about the father constantly trashing the mother while in his presence. The father saw the mother's behavior as her rage at him for having "dumped" her and taken away a privileged life. The father was, in fact, projecting his own anger onto the mother and saw it as hers. Because he could then see her as a vindictive, ruthless, Olympic-quality player of the game of "keep away," it was easy for him to justify his behavior toward her. Most frightening to the observer was his chasing her down a steep mountain road, at high speed, with their 5-year-old son in the front seat of her car while he banged his front bumper into the rear of her car. Later, as he talked about the incident, he was oblivious to the fact that he had put his son in grave danger. His focus was that she needed to be punished for attempting, once again, to keep his son away from him. His assumption was that the son also believed the father's distortion. This distortion through projection was so grave that he mentally placed the boy in the seat beside himself and did not consider the son's terror from being in a rear-ended car with his frightened mother.

As people descend to this third level of narcissistic injury, the ability to tolerate an opinion different from their own gradually diminishes to a point where no differing opinion can be accepted. Individuals at this level see those who disagree with them as either being "in denial," stupid, or in collusion with the other party. No shades of gray are permitted—one is either "for me" or "against me." As people descend the levels, they increasingly view themselves as "victims." As victims, and thereby acted upon by external, uncontrollable forces, they assume a hypervigilant, reactive stance. When the power in the relationship is placed with the other partner, victims learn little from experience because they do not see themselves as responsible for the situation. Their stance is one of "if you would only stop doing what you are doing, then I could stop doing what I am doing." Sometimes victims present as helpless and passive because they have not developed an adequate sense of agency—a belief that they can act effectively in the world.

A divorce always conveys a message of failure, which then forces the question of what an individual's part was in the failed marriage. Narcissistically vulnerable people are very susceptible to disturbance and overreaction to this question. Their self-esteem can be unrealistically high or low. They can feel either totally worthless or inflated with self-importance. Rationalizations abound in the form of saying, "I used to always feel to blame, but now I know she was the flawed person and I was just an innocent victim of her machinations." In divorce, the problems with self-esteem in narcissistically vulnerable people arise from their inability to tolerate internal conflict or ambivalence toward themselves or others in their lives. Ambivalence is a human universal. No one is perfect, even those we love the most. If flaws or weaknesses are seen as "bad," then a narcissistically vulnerable person is threatened with the loss of an illusion of being nearly perfect. In addition, their children then must be seen as good because the behavior of children is seen as a reflection of parenting ability. Thus, projection again arises because children's flaws must be laid at someone else's feet. "It is her mother's fault that my daughter is doing so poorly in school because her mother never checks her homework." If it is the other parent who is responsible for the children's problems, then there is justification for controlling that parent's access to the children.

It is important to note that "narcissistically vulnerable" is not synonymous with the clinical diagnosis of a narcissistic personality disorder. Narcissistic vulnerability has to do with a person's previous life experiences, their spoken and unconscious assumptions about marriage and intimacy, and their ability to accept responsibility as well as to tolerate psychological pain. How an individual manages the narcissistic wounds of the divorce can be used as one indicator that a high-conflict divorce and post-divorce situation is likely. The following list presents some helpful guidelines for identifying a narcissistically vulnerable individual at risk of contributing to a high-conflict divorce (Kopetski 1991):

1. *One parent is seen as having a serious potential to harm the children.* There are unrealistic and unfounded fears that one parent does not have an ability to care for the children without endangerment. This parent has a *fear* that is treated as a reality. The reality is presented so convincingly and vividly that the listener is seduced into believing it is a reality rather than a simple fear. A typical example is the parent who believes the other parent will drink and drive with the children. Although the other parent does drink, there is no evidence of drinking and driving; but there is a fear of that happening in the parent's mind. The fear is treated as if it were a reality. Although, in our judicial system, one is innocent until proven guilty, a deeply wounded parent, with justification for revenge, can be very convincing. The argument is very seductive, as well as being professionally threatening, because it calls for a judgment which, if wrong, could be dangerous to a child and guilt inducing to the professional.

2. *The wounded parent gives the children a distorted, negative perception of the other parent.* In its most blatant form this represents a negative campaign to poison the children's minds against the other parent. A powerful sign that can be observed is children sounding like miniature adults with a glib, matter-of-fact quality to their presentations.

More frequently it is the parent who makes continuous
off-hand remarks or invidious comparisons in the course
of normal conversation. To the dispassionate observer the
remarks often seem gratuitous such as "Your mother
never really wanted you," or "I tried so hard to get your
dad to play ball with you, but he was lazy and just didn't
care about you enough." Essentially the mention of the
other parent's name always has a negative qualifier that
often, in itself, is not overwhelming but mounts up to a
very negative force if one hears it day in and day out. One
teenager who managed to survive the conflict by immers-
ing himself in his peer group laughingly observed (albeit
with an undercurrent of sadness), "My mother now has
two new names if you listen to my dad, now it's 'your
mother, *the bitch.*'"

3. *The wounded parent talks to and treats the children as if the
   children were peers.* Many wounded parents have telephone
   conversations or conversations with friends or relatives in
   the presence of the children so the children can overhear.
   An improperly drawn boundary becomes apparent, in
   that a circle is drawn around the parent and the children
   to the exclusion of the other parent and anyone else who
   may disagree. Look for the phenomenon of *parentification,*
   in which the children become a substitute for the missing
   other parent. For example, a father may make a 15-year-
   old daughter into his official hostess and tell her that she
   is much more fun than her mother, who never liked large
   parties.

4. *The wounded parent directly expresses a desire to limit or exclude
   contact with the other parent.* Usually such statements are
   justified by the wounded parent saying that there is a good
   reason for the exclusion and listing the other parent's
   high crimes and misdemeanors. Typical accusations include that the parent lives in an inadequate apartment
   and/or in a dangerous part of town, or that the other

parent is merely taking the children for spite and will leave them with a girlfriend or relative when the children could, in fact, be cared for in a loving, attentive, and parent-present home. Accusations, of course, can be much more savage. Again, the PC must have some way to explore the veracity of the report so as to determine if fear is being turned into a reality.

5. *The wounded parent claims an entitlement or some other method of redressing an injustice.* Entitlement means assuming a position of expecting certain benefits or privileges. A simple example of this is the statement that the other parent, who does not pay child support, should not be allowed to see the children because the person who supports the children "owns" the children. The statement is not usually put so blatantly, but careful examination will reveal that the entitlement of ownership is the underlying premise. Another example would be a marriage of mixed religions in which the wounded parent claims total control of religious education because his or her religion demands it (in their eyes).

A careful listener should be able to differentiate between the use of allegations versus accusations. An accusation, particularly when rigidly fixed, is warning that there is potential for high conflict. An allegation states a parental concern or worry that is open to the receipt of new information. With an accusation, the only information accepted is information that affirms the parent's closely held opinion. The parent's belief system is not open to new, opposing information. For instance, in a divorce there can be allegations or accusations of sexual abuse. The parent who makes an allegation will often hope that the issue is not true and will be relieved when well-documented information comes forth saying that nothing has happened. An accuser, on the other hand, will not accept information that does not confirm the accusation. This can be seen, for instance, in therapist or doctor shopping—a situation in which accusing parents move from one professional to the next until they find one who agrees with their view. The unfortunate case of a small girl being vaginally examined by five doctors for evidence of sexual abuse is an example of this. Whoever disagrees with the accusing parent is seen as being either "in denial" or "bought" by the other parent, so any continuing collaboration is dismissed because it will only continue the injustice. The wounded parent presents as fighting against overwhelming forces to nobly protect the children in a sea of hostility and indifference. Be suspicious when any parent begins to strap on their shining armor so as to serve the children.

DEFENSIVE STYLES
IN HIGH-CONFLICT PERSONALITIES

To regain the equilibrium of self-esteem, many psychological defenses can be used. One that is nearly always present is the projection of blame. It is important to recognize how projection of blame can be presented when one is working with a person in a high-conflict post-divorce situation. Three defensive styles that are commonly encountered include (Garrity and Baris 1994):

I Am Always Right. These are individuals who have the absolute serenity of knowing they are always right. Such individuals are highly self-focused and think of themselves as possessing "The Truth." One is immediately aware of being in their presence when one hears the same thing from them again and again, only louder each time. They behave like characters from the old comedy movie scene where the American tourist keeps asking the same questions of the native in a louder and louder voice, as if they were deaf and that was the reason they were not understanding. "Always right" clients have a highly inflated view of themselves. A normal sense of competence is pumped up to overconfidence to such a level that they will bear no argument. Such individuals are often attractive to insecure people who are looking for shelter under the wing of someone who, with great confidence, makes decisions easily. The backgrounds of such individuals often include a string of failed relationships because they lack the capacity to learn from their mistakes, because, by definition, they do not make mistakes—other people make mistakes. Life is then seen as a series of involvements with flawed people who just could not "get it right."

Watch for the client who enters the office with a record of having worked with a number of highly competent professionals and each relationship has failed and been abandoned. A long shopping list of professionals often signals that professional competence is measured in terms of *agreement with* the client's position.

Spousal abuse can occur in these marriages. It reflects the "always right" people reaching the outer limits of frustration because no matter how right they were and how loudly they spoke, their partner did not comply. Abuse often takes the form of unpremeditated explosions as the frustration tolerance falls low because the partner simply will not behave. As a parent coordinator, one arena of required artistry when working with this type of client is the ability to find face-saving ways to help the client abandon a position. Often it can be done by feeding their self-importance in offering them a self-enhancing alternative to their "always right" position. For instance, a father was convinced that his daughter's mother was pumping her full of Ritalin on certain public occasions so as to drug her into passivity. He insisted that the administration of all medications be done by him, because he knew how to do it. It was suggested that the child's pediatrician be put in charge of counting pills and making a statement as to how long they should last, so the mother, with whom the child lived, could still administer the pills but she would be "watched" by the pediatrician. The father readily accepted because it appealed to his sense of the mother's massive incompetence because now a professional had been brought in to monitor her. The mother, in fact, was happy with the plan because it got the father off her back and she felt very comfortable in the working relationship with the pediatrician.

My Ex-Spouse Is Always Wrong. If the always right person represents the epitome of inflated self-importance and self-love, the "you are always wrong" person reflects the epitome of projection of blame. These are often angry, overcontrolled people who are not very pleasant to be around. They provide a litany of the high crimes and misdemeanors of the ex-partner and usually speak of these crimes with the spirit and relish of a person who truly enjoys collecting them. A dead giveaway is listening to their recitation and believing the transgressions happened within the recent past only to find, upon inquiry, that the events took place three or four years previously. By holding the ex-partner at fault, such an individual completely protects himself from culpability and, therefore, from a sense of guilt or shame for having done something wrong. These people live in and for the past. Usually they easily gain an upper hand as the chronicler of crimes by flooding the PC with court transcripts, police reports, driving records, and testimonials from witnesses and friends. If one enters the past in the company of such a biased guide, one can only be caught up in the high crime, punitive mind-set. The best way to deal with such individuals is to attempt to lead them from the past to the present. Attacking defenses, or mounting a counterargument that things did not take place as stated three years ago, dooms a PC to failure because it appears as if the criminal ex-spouse is being defended. Even a hint that the PC is joining with the enemy prompts a fight. A present and future orientation is often helpful in eliciting compromise or cooperation from this type of person. Pointing out that regardless of past crimes, there is a current problem to be solved can be very helpful in loosening the person from his or her preoccupation with the past to problem solving in the here and now. The client with this resolution for shoring up self-esteem is particularly difficult to work with because the anger against the other parent is pervasive and can be seductive. When the PC is constantly bathed in the rage of a client, he or she must be very careful not to get caught up in it and either join with or act out against the blaming client.

Maybe I Will, Maybe I Won't. A third self-esteem adjustment is that of the client whose anger bobs underground and aboveground. Garrity and Baris call them *Maybe I Will and Maybe I Won't* (MIW/MIW) clients. While their anger is not constant, it is very close to the surface and it bobs up at the slightest provocation. One author likens it to trying to put an octopus in a coffee can. You think you have it all contained and then a tentacle slithers out. Such clients are characteristically very unfocused. It is difficult to understand the structure of their logic and to see the points of light in all the heat that gets generated by their anger. They can be most frustrating to work with because they waffle, with the waffling driven by the bobbing of their anger. A PC may feel that a problem has been resolved and a compromise reached, only to find a phone call on voice mail the next morning that says, "I've changed my mind." As Garrity and Baris (1994) point out, "Disappointing other's expectations seems to give them a sense of control" (p. 117). MIW/MIW clients, through their constantly changing positions, are difficult to pin down. By not being pinned down, they escape being trapped and possibly being engulfed or held to and criticized for their viewpoint. Like a rabbit zigzagging across a field to escape a pursuing fox, the positional zigzag of MIW/MIW clients keeps them safe because it both keeps others constantly off balance and keeps them from being pinned down and criticized. Their motto is "Come closer, farther away," and they are enormously sensitive to issues of interpersonal distance between people. They are challenging to work with because a PC will rarely know what will set them off. What can be helpful is to explain to them what an issue under discussion might bring up. It is akin to programs put on by hospitals for young children where the children are brought to the hospital for a walk-through to see what the operating room looks like, where they will sleep, etc. A preliminary walk through with the PC flagging flashpoints can sometimes be helpful. The "dress rehearsal" can often identify emotional reactions, so when they occur the client can recognize them and not be carried away by them. It also joins the PC with the client so that when a PC senses a client beginning to react to a previously identified flashpoint, a look, a gesture, or a time-out can help the client not feel alone and gain control of their feelings.

The above three defensive postures, which represent the use of narcissistic activity to regain self-esteem, can be seen as falling along a continuum. At the far left sit people who adjust by thinking of themselves as "perfect," as having all the answers and whose main job is to bring others into the fold of their perfectly reasonable thinking. At the far right of the continuum are the "you are always wrong" people who externalize and project all blame onto others. Whereas the "I am right" people hold themselves blameless, the "You are wrong" people do not puff themselves up so much as they bring other persons down. Somewhere in the middle are the MIW/MIW people who dodge and feint, depending on how accessible their anger is. Sometimes they accept, but often they reject as they strive not to take a position that will open them to being pinned down and thus assailable.

Typically the spouses of any of these defensive-style individuals have a terrible time working out a cooperative divorce arrangement. They may remind one of a gored bull, standing in confusion in a noisy stadium with little clue as to what hit them or what to do about it. They are often surrounded by experts who tell them what to do, but functioning in that kind of mode always places them in a reactive rather then proactive mode. They are proverbially "a day late and a dollar short" in the transactions with the other parent. For instance, a "You are always wrong" mother arranged through a PC that she, living out of state, could call her sons every night between eight and nine o'clock. After a while, she started calling at about 8:50 P.M. and insisted on keeping the children on the phone for her full hour. After all, the time slot gave her an hour to talk to the children (between eight and nine o'clock), but also gave her a window of time to contact, between 8:00 P.M. and 9:00 P.M. No one anticipated her creative and self-serving distortion of the intent of the rule. The father dithered terribly and simply could not set a limit on her even though having his elementary school-age children staying up to ten o'clock upset him greatly. He felt that the children needed to talk to their mother and he knew that their mother would raise a ruckus if he limited her, so he was skewered on the horns of ambivalence and could not move. He was a passive and compliant man who had few assertiveness skills. If passive people try to become assertive with these defensive styles, even in the most appropriate ways, they often elicit a firestorm of pressure to go back to their old, passive ways. Pair any of the above three defensive styles with an easily victimized spouse and one can begin to imagine the control dances that take place with the PC.

In summary, the dynamics of a high-conflict divorce situation are complex. There are some people who have such strong needs to maintain control that there may be endless arguments about the color of invitations to a bar mitzvah or whether a child is allowed to drive at night. This is a small subpopulation of post-divorce high conflict. Of greater concern are those who are defending against the pain of feeling inadequate or harmed by the divorce. Vulnerability to being narcissistically wounded depends on one's life experiences in terms of adequacy and lovability. The more the maintenance of self-esteem is externally placed, the more vulnerable an individual is to narcissistic wounds. When the vulnerability is great and the wound is deep, individuals move through a series of self-soothing postures to help shore up self-esteem. One defensive posture involves taking the disturbing feelings and placing or "projecting" them onto someone else so these feelings are seen as external. Defending against the onslaughts of a demon is much more socially acceptable and psychologically comfortable than dealing with one's own demons inside, which represent flaws. Wounded people attempt to recover by thinking of themselves as being okay.

The narcissistic assault generated by divorce may create a distorted perception of reality and of boundaries between people. The distortions arise from a need for self-protection in the service of maintaining self-esteem. Boundaries can be drawn inappropriately in two ways. One is to draw a circle around oneself with the result of seeing others as objects. There is a profound lack of empathy for others, in this instance, as it is empathy that helps bridge boundaries. Another maladaptive distortion of boundaries involves a circle drawn about the children and the parent together that not only excludes the other parent but makes the children and the parent one. This perception, when extreme, motivates a wounded parent to exclude the other parent from the children's lives and surround himself/herself only with people who agree. A distorted yet supportive atmosphere is then created in which the wounded parent has justification for acting to exclude or significantly control the other parent's access to the children. Indicators of this mind-set are the expressed views that the other parent is harmful to the children and that the children should be directly informed of the harmfulness of that other parent. The children may be elevated to the role of companions and peers, and it is argued that there is justification for removing the other parent from the children's lives. Furthermore, there is an assertion that accusations of harmfulness are true and only the biased, those in collusion with the other parent, or those "in denial," would hold otherwise and thus perpetuate the damage to the children.

Understanding the dynamics of high-conflict couples can provide a helpful framework for planning interventions because with a foundation of theoretical knowledge it is easier to understand what to do as well as what *not* to do. BeaLisa Sydlik (1999), in a briefing paper prepared for the Oregon Judicial Department, noted that researchers and practitioners find several dimensions to operationalize conflict, some of which are "normal." "Normal" high conflict, she explained, "can be expected right at the time immediately following separation, when emotions and the degree of disruption are still high. As the family adjusts, and wounds heal, this normal conflict may dissipate to varying degrees, allowing the family to restructure as the parents find a way to continue parenting after divorce. This is to be compared with the more intractable conflict, which commonly takes place post-decree. It is this protracted high conflict that is indicative of preexisting psychological and family dysfunction and which is more resistant to legal and therapeutic interventions." According to Johnston and Campbell (1988), "Children in highly conflicted divorce are two to five times more likely to be clinically disturbed in emotions and behavior compared with national norms. Many of these factors are hypothesized to be reciprocally related to each other" (p. 173).

The importance of being able to identify and intervene with the high-conflict dynamics becomes paramount in terms of protection of children of divorce. Increasingly it is noted that there needs to be a greater array of services targeting the different areas of conflict provided to families functioning at different levels of post-divorce conflict. Domestic violence exists at the extreme end of the scale; however, elements of conflict and contentiousness exist throughout the spectrum of separation and divorce. It is important, thus, for clinicians, attorneys, parent coordinators, or others dealing with or delivering services to these families to distinguish the nature and intensity of the conflict to appropriately structure services for a given family.

Jennifer Barker and her group of mediators in Vermont, who have organized a parent-coordination program, find that the degree of structure, the intensity of services, the number of professionals involved, and the number of professional roles that need to be involved must be increased as conflict increases. The necessity for keeping couples apart when the conflict has been protracted and when repeated and recent physical abuse has taken place is paramount. The Vermont group has adopted Garrity and Baris (1994) Conflict Assessment Scale (Table 2–2), which divides domestic disputes into categories of minimal, mild, moderate, moderately severe, and severe. Other states, such as Idaho, Arizona, and Georgia, have adopted the use of this instrument or others similar to it. If the level of conflict can be identified early, then appropriate intervention can be determined, be that a parent coordinator, supervised visitation, or a traditional mediation process. Often parent education classes are helpful as well.

Note that parents may move up and down the Conflict Assessment Scale (Garrity and Baris 1994), changing categories as the conflict hopefully diminishes over time. Sometimes with the addition of a new spouse or other changing circumstances, a couple may move up on the Conflict Assessment Scale as well.

TABLE 2–2. CONFLICT ASSESSMENT SCALE

Minimal	Mild	Moderate	Moderately Severe	Severe
• Cooperative parenting	• Occasionally berates other parent in front of child	• Verbal abuse with no threat or history of physical violence	• Child is not directly endangered but parents are endangering to each other	• Endangerment by physical or sexual abuse
• Ability to separate children's needs from own needs	• Occasional verbal quarreling in front of child	• Loud quarreling	• Threatening violence	• Drug or alcohol abuse to point of impairment
• Can validate importance of other parent	• Questioning child about personal matters in life of other parent	• Denigration of other parent	• Slamming doors, throwing things	• Severe psychological pathology
• Can affirm the competency of other parent	• Occasional attempts to form a coalition with child against other parent	• Threatens to limit access of other parent	• Verbally threatening harm or kidnapping	
• Conflict is resolved between the adults using verbal exchange with only occasional expressions of anger		• Threats of litigation	• Continual litigation	
• Negative emotions quickly brought under control		• Ongoing attempts to form a coalition with child against other parent around isolated issues	• Attempts to form a permanent or standing coalition with child against other parent (alienation syndrome)	
			• Child is experiencing emotional endangerment	

3

How Children Cope with High Conflict

Parents who remain entrenched in high conflict over a long period of time may be sacrificing their children's future well-being. The most powerful determining factor in good adult outcome for children of divorce is the level and intensity of the parental conflict. Aggression, behavior problems, and depression are frequent early responses to being caught in the middle of animosity between parents. Being in the middle ranges from hearing one parent berate the other to vicious, verbal attacks; from threats of violence to actual violence; or from subtle pleas for loyalty to explicit demands to openly side with one parent. All conflict hurts, and the more intense, pervasive, and open the hostility is, the greater the toll it can take on the children.

Most divorcing parents battle furiously during the first year of separation. For half of them, disputes will involve physical violence even when this was not present in the marriage. By the second year, most couples begin to settle into a post-divorce arrangement, and by the third year, those who have disengaged and begun to heal emotionally minimize their conflict. Consequently, it can be assumed that couples who are still in intense conflict two to three years post separation are likely to remain in conflict and the children are at risk (Maccoby and Mnookin 1992).

AGE AND DEVELOPMENTAL STAGES

It is important to understand, in some detail, how conflict between parents is experienced by children of various ages and levels of maturity. Children cope with divorce according to fairly consistent age patterns. They also handle interparental conflict differently at different ages. Research indicates that these age differences depend principally on an ability to understand the content of arguments, overall maturity, internal resources, and the availability of support systems (Johnston and Campbell 1988).

Preverbal/Preschoolers

Young children who are preverbal or preschoolers typically manifest extraordinary distress when exposed to parental fighting. They feel the heightened emotion, react to the angry tone of the voices, and sense that something is very wrong. Children at this age panic, look distressed much of the time, and regress in their skill development. Some become withdrawn or overly aggressive. The most serious of all are the children who become severely disorganized and lose their normal developmental milestones.

Four to Five Years of Age

Four- to five-year-old children are old enough to take in elements of parental conflict but they fail to understand the overall context of their parents' arguments and disharmony. The tendency of children at this age is to ask very concrete questions about what they have overheard or seen. They also worry about their basic needs being met or feel that it is their job to soothe an upset parent. Believing they are all-powerful, these children often expect to be able to fix the problem. When they learn, over time, that they cannot change the situation, they begin to doubt their own competency and to develop mistrust in the world. Emotional disorganization and confusion may occur. Some of these young children experience the most profound distress and panic, and lose confidence that they can control their world.

Elementary Age

Early elementary school-aged children have a broader cognitive understanding of the conflict between their parents but are not yet able to integrate the two different points of view. Consequently, children of this age group cope by reflecting the point of view of the parent they are with at the moment. This can actually escalate the conflict between the parents as each hears the children report something completely opposite. Sadly, some of these children disconnect from their own feelings as a way to please parents, and they become increasingly unable to develop a sense of how they actually feel. Children who polarize themselves in this fashion and learn to deny their own feelings and desires to preserve ties to each parent gradually lose a sense of who they are.

Preteen

By the preteen years, children are fully capable of understanding the conflict between their parents. They often demand adult-level explanations of the difficulties. These children are becoming increasingly moralistic and idealistic and tend to form judgments about who is right and who is wrong. They may side strongly with one parent while rejecting the other. Sometimes these children begin to act on these judgments by refusing to visit a parent or remaining rude, aloof, and uncommunicative during visits.

Adolescents

Adolescents who must cope with high conflict between parents are unpredictable. Some teenagers who made up their minds at age 10 or 11 to exclude one parent from their lives never change and continue to exclude that parent. Other teenagers are independent and may take a sudden interest in a mother or father they have not seen for years. Adolescence can be a second chance, an opportunity to heal old wounds and to create new relationships. With an ability to act independently, teenagers can make calls, write letters, or visit without the other parent being aware of the interest. It is a fortunate parent who finds his or her adolescent reaching out to forge a new parent–child bond. Adolescents' interest in relationships with the opposite sex is often affected by their perceptions of their parents' marriages.

LONG-TERM OUTCOME

Two prominent research teams have studied what happens to children's personality styles after years of exposure to interparental conflict. Johnston and Campbell (1988) define four main personality styles that emerge: maneuvering, equilibrating, merging, and diffusing.

The "maneuvering" personality is a style adopted by children who become more or less master manipulators. These are children who have learned how to get parents to argue, which shifts the focus of conflict away from them. They learn how to meet their own needs. These children learn essentially how to look out for number one through years of negotiating their way through interparental squabbling. These children are very adept at meeting their own needs but, sadly, tend to form shallow attachments to others.

Another style, "equilibrating," describes children who are excellent diplomats. While they appear to manifest little anxiety of their own, they are capable of tolerating a high degree of conflict. They respond by acting as mediators and managers of the conflict between their parents. Channeled in the right direction, maintaining equanimity and managing conflict around very powerful others experiencing high-conflict struggles may be an enhancing trait. There is evidence that these people are perennially anxious, even though their external demeanor appears calm.

The next personality style described by Johnston and Campbell is the "merging" type. This group is characterized by children who manifest a fair degree of sadness and a degree of vacancy that is perceptible in interactions with them. This group comprises children who are caught at the 6- to 8-year-old developmental level of coping with conflict. These are children who are no longer in touch with their own feelings but seem, in an empty manner, to reflect the feelings of those around them. They look externally for others to define their own internal feeling states. This is a mechanism adopted in order to cope, as these children do not possess diplomatic skills. The children get drawn into arguments and essentially merge themselves with one parent, the other, or both, continually taking sides in the ongoing conflict.

The fourth maladaptive coping style is the "diffusing" type. Sadly, these are the children who shatter emotionally. They fail to develop adequate defenses to protect themselves against the interparental warfare. These are the children who literally fall apart and do not function in day-to-day life and activities. They may require institutionalization to gain the external structure necessary to fully develop their personalities. This is the group that Johnston and Campbell identify as the most dysfunctional and disorganized.

More recently, Johnston (Johnston and Roseby 1997) identified a number of areas of grave concern for children who grow up amidst the daily reality of parental conflict:

1. An undermining of moral growth due to differing realities of right and wrong presented by their parents.
2. The lack of a foundation and belief in their own competence.
3. A tendency to oversimplify and distort information from others so as to maintain their own view.

Over time, these children close off access to inner experiences as well as interpersonal relationships that promote maturity and healthy development. Needing to protect themselves and maintain control, the children of high-conflict divorces sacrifice spontaneity, flexibility, and the development of a genuine sense of self.

Psychologist and researcher E. Mavis Hetherington (Hetherington et al. 1989) from the University of Virginia also notes the existence of identifiable personality styles of children exposed to long-term interparental conflict. She identifies one of these styles as "aggressive and insecure," a group in which there are three times as many boys as girls. Children adopting this style tended to model after highly aggressive, volatile parents. Seventy percent of this group reported that they could not sustain close friendships and manifested aggressive and impulsive behavior both at school and at home.

Hetherington, however, notes other more optimistic characterizations of some of the children who came out of high-conflict homes. She categorizes one of her identifiable types as "opportunistic and competent." This group parallels to some extent Johnston and Campbell's (1988) "equilibrating" personalities. These children are able to be very influential and calming, even when there are very powerful people around them manifesting a high degree of conflict. They are diplomatic and able to make friends easily. They have difficulty, however, in maintaining relationships over time and in depth, although on the surface they are engaging and charming.

The third group that Hetherington was able to identify is a group she calls "caring-competent." Optimistically, she identifies this group as being as well adjusted as many of the children who grew up in intact families in which there were not ongoing battles. Very often these children have been expected to do caretaking of siblings. Girls growing up in the custody of a single-parent mother figure seem to manifest this style. Children falling into this category do well in terms of establishing genuine relationships and caring and empathic positions with others.

All children who grow up in high-conflict situations are not condemned to personality disturbances. Many factors contribute to the adult outcome of children in high-conflict divorce situations. As with all trauma, some children do surprisingly well, and researchers have increasingly looked to these children to understand the factors inherent in recovery and resilience.

Little research has been done on the length of time parents spent in negative interactional patterns before they reached a decision to divorce. Certainly, most children of divorce have long histories of exposure to high levels of parental conflict before the divorce occurs. Some researchers (Block et al. 1988) have found evidence of children's distress as long as eleven years prior to the divorce. A longitudinal study conducted in Great Britain in the 1970s followed a large group of children from ages 7 to 11. Typically, the children whose parents had divorced by the time they were age 11 were doing less well than those who remained in intact families. The surprise, however, was that when the earlier data were examined, these same children were in distress four years earlier while their families were still intact. For boys especially, this study found that the divorce itself did not appear to be as large a contributing factor as the pre-divorce family environment (Cherlin et al. 1991).

Although the link between interparental conflict and a capacity to cope is complex and multidetermined, some children demonstrate remarkable resiliency and capacity to seek protective relationships outside the family. These children demonstrate good interpersonal adjustment, self-esteem, and coping. Other children, however, appear to succumb to the conflict between their parents. Boys are most at risk to externalize and model their parents' ineffective problem-solving style by becoming aggressive with peers, whereas girls are more likely to internalize distress and to suffer from anxiety and depression. Four factors have been considered to be primary determinants of children's adjustment: (1) modeling of an ineffective problem-solving style by the parents both pre- and post-divorce; (2) emotional dysregulation within the children as a result of living in a tension-filled environment; (3) feeling responsible for the conflict; and (4) disruption of the relationship between each parent and the children. Most researchers agree that there is a definite link between parental conflict and children's adjustment, but more long-term studies are needed to fully understand the pathways by which these factors impact children. The ages of the children, the resiliency of the children's personalities, and the capacity to have and to seek out protective influences are all important mitigating factors in living with tension and hostility between parents (Emery and Forehand 1994).

Recently, clinicians and researchers alike have been taking a closer look at those children who do cope successfully, who grow from the adversity in their lives, and who maintain optimism in spite of their difficult circumstances (Katz 1997, Rutter 1987, Seligman 1996). Factors that are emerging as protective ones for children of divorce include:

1. *A supportive relationship with at least one parent* (Camara and Resnick 1987, Gelman 1991). This appears to provide

children with a secure base, a buffer against abandonment fears, and a haven of protection from which to draw
strength.

2. *The presence of siblings.* Siblings frequently support and
communicate with one another during times of stress as
well as buffer one another from the exposure to parental
conflict, which a single child must endure alone. Children
with siblings have been found to have a more realistic view
of the parents' divorce and less of a sense of having been
the cause of the divorce (Cowen et al. 1990, Kempton et
al. 1991).

3. *Supportive caretakers in the role of grandparents, teachers,
friends, and day-care providers.* The degree of nurturing
social support available to children outside the family
arena is highly associated with good adjustment post-
divorce. Both the quantity and the quality of the time
spent with outside social support are important variables
(Katz 1997). These outside affectional ties encourage
initiative as these other adults recognize the accomplish-
ments of the children with their hobbies and interests,
which in turn bolsters a sense of pride.

4. *Group therapy, especially when the focus is on providing information, sharing feelings, and developing coping skills.*

Thus, protective factors can be characterized in three dimensions: those that originate within the children, such as resiliency
and problem-solving skills; those that originate from a family
member, such as one well-functioning parent, a brother, a sister,
or an extended family member; and finally, those that originate
from within the community, such as a neighbor, teacher, or
supportive therapist. Not only can these protective factors immu-
nize children against the conflict in divorce, but they also appear
to provide overall protection in life against adversities of all kinds.

Recently, two outstanding books have attracted the attention
of parents and professionals, encouraging them to allow children

to struggle with life's challenges and to provide them with the tools to face these challenges—tools such as self-regulation, optimism, empathy, and social connection to others (Daniel Goleman's *Emotional Intelligence* [1995]; Martin Seligman's *The Optimistic Child* [1996]). Divorce can be framed many ways. The wise parent is one who does not deny the pain, loss, and anger, but who also does not sink into depression and pessimism because of it. Life can and will go on, and many children of divorce manage to live the phrase written by Robert Louis Stevenson and used by Mark Katz for the title of his recent book: "Life is not so much a matter of holding good cards, but sometimes of playing a poor hand well."

Part II

Elements of High-Conflict Management

The Parenting Coordinator (PC) can provide a communication link, foster relationship building, represent the needs of the children, contain the destructive conflict, and ease everyone into a healthier, more civilized post-divorce adjustment directed toward growth and recovery.

As the Parenting Coordinator begins to work with a family, it is important to keep in mind that, by this point, the family may well have dealt with a number of other experts who have failed to help them to fully reduce their conflict. Their experiences have likely been that of a succession of attorneys, therapists, Guardians *ad litem*, and so on. They are likely to have an intense curiosity about how the PC, as a new professional, will function. The family will be sensitive to any signs that indicate the PC's convictions and tendencies.

Often, in the very beginning of a situation, the PC will be immediately confronted with a crisis, that is, something that needs to be decided "this instant." This can be an attempt to flush out the position of the PC to enable the family to assess the position that the PC will take vis-à-vis the family and one or the other parent. It is critical that mediation and/or arbitration not begin until there has been sufficient time to evaluate the situation and to have some sense of the dynamics that drive it.

Whereas an attorney is required to vigorously pursue the interests of only his client, and often the individual therapist, whether willingly and consciously or inadvertently, becomes an advocate for his or her client's positional point of view, a Parenting Coordinator has a different job. The PC's main focus is the relationship between the parents and the well-being of the child as his/her client. The PC helps the parents make joint decisions or the PC needs to make decisions in his/her arbitration function quickly and efficiently. The focus then is to observe the dynamics of the parental system as it changes over the course of the work done with the family. Making decisions before one knows the parental system is frequently an invitation to disaster. If the PC's interventions are to be successful, there must be an alliance with each of the parents. The alliance need not say "I agree with your perception of reality," but, rather, "I understand your perception of reality."

One of the most difficult transitions to make from either the mental health or the legal profession to performing the PC function is that of holding back the challenge to the perception of the parent who has been perpetuating the conflict by manifesting the mentality of "if you are not for me, you are against me." Challenging the closely held assumption that the ex-spouse is a monster will bring the PC down in ringing defeat because if one does not agree, then one is the enemy. The difficult thing to do as a PC is to understand that the client perceives the other as a monster while not agreeing that the other parent is, indeed, a monster. The artistry of being a PC is to simultaneously understand why a client will see the other parent in a certain way but also to say, "I see it differently," and not make it sound like a challenge to the defenses of the client. Janet Johnston (Johnston and Campbell 1988) uses a phrase such as, "Thank you for sharing your experience, and I will be keeping my eyes open for that."

An example of not challenging a client's defenses is one in which a mother, who had spent a lifetime with her children on welfare, was again resisting a reasonable request for her to get help in controlling her children. Although this example is not drawn from a high-conflict couple, it demonstrates the point about not engaging defenses. The client had spent many years sabotaging the many treatment plans offered by Social Services to the court, and essentially she was very system-wise. A therapist was assigned to help her develop parenting techniques that might help her keep the children under better control. She deeply resented the therapy requirement because it made her feel that everyone thought she was a bad mother. Her perception was accurate. In her resistance to the parenting intervention, she announced to the therapist with all sincerity that she did not have to be helped to anticipate her children's behavior because *she could read their minds.* In the past, such statements would have prompted the professional to challenge her, and any forward momentum would have been blocked. The therapist, although anxious about what he was about to do, told her it was wonderful if she could read her children's minds, because if she could, there would be no need for training in anticipating what they *might* do—she knew what they were *going* to do! The woman was startled by the response, then very pleased that someone recognized, in essence, that she was a good mother. The rest of parent training honored her ability to read their minds, while helping her develop a concept of behavioral consequences for her children. The mother's defense of mind reading was not challenged, and therefore she did not lose face or hear that she was a bad mother. Her self-esteem intact, she could move into the arena of improving already good parenting skills. The therapist was anxious about the treatment ploy because of an uneasy feeling of possibly agreeing to a true distortion. However, by not engaging the defense that created the resistance, an end run around the defense was made and cooperation was elicited.

Despite a couple's clamoring for a quick decision on an issue, it is best to first undertake an explanation of the PC process, the signing of a clear contract, and an assessment phase. This initial evaluation process also serves as a relationship foundation with clients. They will feel they have been able to tell their stories, have been listened to, and have someone who understands how they feel.

One of the most difficult concepts for the PC to grasp is that there is probably no one decision that will make the conflict go away. The conflict over a particular issue may end, but conflict will arise someplace else. One PC realized that PC survival is predicated not so much on making the *right* decision but, rather, on making a *good* decision. The differentiation is between searching for a decision that will end the conflict and searching for a decision that would serve the best interests of the children at that particular moment. It is not unusual for the PC to feel that no one is pleased with a decision, and frequently any decision made by somebody other than the primary parent is probably not a decision that is easy to accept. Some of the authors joke that if anyone is pleased with a decision, then it is probably the wrong decision. While this is, perhaps, a good example of gallows humor, it ruefully reflects our tendencies as PCs to look for the one *right* decision, even though we know it is elusive, if not nonexistent. For the client, the de-escalation of the conflict comes with the gradual realization that in working with the PC decisions are made as quickly as possible with a minimization of time for conflict to escalate into major impasse.

In dealing with the high-conflict couple, the PC must come to understand the way each sees the world and, in particular, the way each conceptualizes the dangerous behavior of the other. Frontal assault on a client's defensive system will usually not work and tends to make that person want to escape the PC process or actively sabotage the PC's ability to effectively intervene. A PC is thus constrained by the client's defenses. Instead of being able to say, "Your view of your spouse as a Machiavellian schemer is simply not true, and the sooner you let go of that image the better you will be able to co-parent your children," the PC is limited to saying, "I know you view your spouse as diabolical, but how will you deal with him for the next twelve years?" It is also possible to challenge a parent's distorted perception with a statement such as, "I know you're concerned that your children are not safe with their father. I haven't seen any evidence of that, but I'll keep my eyes open."

FUNCTIONS OF THE PARENTING COORDINATOR

The PC has four functions or spheres of activity: assessment, education, interfacing, and intervention. Each of these functions is very important, but the particular role that a PC plays in a situation needs to be tailored by the PC to his or her own expertise and style as well as to the particular needs of the family. Associated with each function of the PC are particular areas that should be considered as the PC begins to work with the family. Table II–1 summarizes the functions and the associated issues to consider.

TABLE II–1.
PARENTING COORDINATOR FUNCTIONS AND ISSUES

The PC can do the following:	The PC should consider these issues:
■ Assess	✥ Interviews
	✥ Marital/Family Impasse
	◆ Parents
	◆ Children
	✥ Information Gathering about Children
	◆ Education
	◆ Health
	◆ Psychological/Emotional Health
	◆ Safety
	◆ Attachment
	◆ Relationship with Each Parent
	✥ Review Custody Evaluation/Study
■ Educate	✥ Conflict Resolution Theory and Techniques
	✥ Child Development
	✥ Communication Skills
	✥ Court/Legal System
	✥ Family Issues
	✥ Resources

■ Interface

- ❖ Family
  - ✦ Parents
  - ✦ Stepparents
  - ✦ Extended
  - ✦ Significant Others
  - ✦ Siblings
- ❖ Systems and Professionals
  - ✦ Mental Health
  - ✦ Social Services
  - ✦ Legal
  - ✦ Education
  - ✦ Law Enforcement
  - ✦ Health Care
  - ✦ Religion

■ Intervene

- ❖ Conflict Management
- ❖ Mediation
- ❖ Arbitration
- ❖ Referral
- ❖ Communication Assistance:
  - ✦ Parent/Parent
  - ✦ Parent/Child
- ❖ Reporting
- ❖ Coaching

4

Assessment

It is important to stress that some level of assessment should occur *before any intervention is undertaken.* Parenting Coordinators (PCs) each have assessment procedures and tools they are particularly fond of and upon which they rely. Why assess? Working with high-conflict couples is like treading through the proverbial mine field. It becomes most important to understand the dynamics of the situation and the kinds of defenses with which the family deals. In such mine fields, the less the PC triggers a defense the more headway is likely to be made in helping a couple break impasses. Conversely, the more often a PC directly challenges the defenses, the more likely it is to escalate the conflict and to lose the couple through the process. It is important to remember that the mind-set of at least one member of the high-conflict couple may fall directly into the binary mode, "if you're not for me, you're against me." Inherent in this assumption is that this person will not associate with anyone seen as being against them. Being a PC is being able to empathize with clients and say that their position is fully understood while simultaneously conveying, in a nonthreatening way, disagreement and dissension with their notion.

ANALYSIS OF THE IMPASSE

Janet Johnston (Johnston and Campbell 1988) suggests three levels of analysis that must be conducted to understand and handle high conflict between couples. We shall refer to them as the tribal issues, the interpersonal issues, and the intrapsychic issues (see Figure 4–1).

Tribal Issues

Often termed "external-social" issues, conflict in tribal issues arises because of the involvement of third parties who are aligned with one of the parents against the other parent. Often each parent has his or her "tribe," or team of backers, who help the parent wage war on the other parent. The team can include family members, lawyers, therapists, schoolteachers, neighbors, and other professionals working with the children and the family. One common example of the external-social sources of impasse is the scenario in which "babies make babies" and the grandparents inherit all the caretaking by trying to raise "both sets of babies." For example, when a teenage couple has a child, it is likely that the grandparents actually raise the child or pay for raising it. Their teenagers are still frequently dependent on their own parents for support and sustenance. When the parents quarrel, the grandparents coach from the sidelines, call plays, and often devise and fund a game plan. Not only must a PC know what the various metaphors are that maintain the conflict, but there must be a plan that includes the grandparents or others of power in

FIGURE 4–1. SOURCES OF DIVORCE IMPASSES

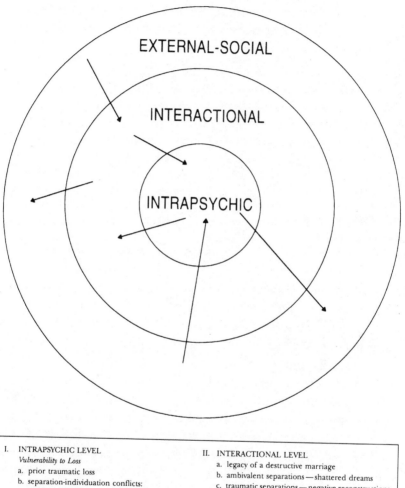

I. INTRAPSYCHIC LEVEL
   Vulnerability to Loss
   a. prior traumatic loss
   b. separation-individuation conflicts:
      diffuse, counter-, and oscillating dependency

   Vulnerability to Humiliation/Shame
   a. mild — specific acknowledgment
   b. moderate — projects total blame
   c. severe — paranoia

II. INTERACTIONAL LEVEL
   a. legacy of a destructive marriage
   b. ambivalent separations — shattered dreams
   c. traumatic separations — negative reconstructions

III. EXTERNAL-SOCIAL LEVEL
   a. tribal warfare
   b. role of mental health professionals/attorneys
   c. role of Court/Judge

This figure is adapted from training material developed by J. R. Johnston and L. E. G. Campbell and is reprinted here with permission. A full explication of this table is available in Johnston and Campbell's book *Impasses of Divorce: The Dynamics and Resolution of Family Conflict*, copyright © 1988 The Free Press.

manipulating the family dynamics, for without their cooperation, intervention is highly likely to fail.

Another common non-nuclear family player is the new stepparent who has ideas as to how the stepchildren should be raised and how co-parenting time should be distributed. It is not unusual for a narcissistically wounded parent to marry a champion, someone who will go out and fight battles, provide a cheering section, or offer strategy and planning support. If this parent is left out of the loop, it will very likely render any impasse resolution attempts to be ineffective. Without the endorsement of all key players, conflict is set up and sabotage ensues.

Interpersonal Issues

A second arena in which to assess the source of impasse is the interactional or interpersonal sphere. This is the "red button analysis." In other words, it is important to understand what interactions are like between the clients and how they trigger one another. This understanding is essential so that the PC does not inadvertently set off a firestorm of conflict by unknowingly choosing inflammatory pathways. The PC should notice in taking the history of the parents that several situations and patterns may suggest that people will continue to press each other's buttons and remain in impasse and that an interactional analysis is a place to start in assessing the situation. Parents who both describe a very destructive marriage that was replete with anger, defensiveness, and emotional abuse are prone to continue that pattern after divorce (an example of a destructive marriage is the one portrayed between George and Martha in Albee's [1988] play, *Who's Afraid of Virginia Woolf*). When parents have had difficulty separating and are ambivalent about the divorce, they may continue the equivocating in the form of acting out so that the other parent remains engaged in the relationship. A sudden abandonment by one of the spouses of the other is often a signal that the parents will play out the abandonment issues in their post-divorce parenting relationship.

By way of illustration, Kevin was the only boy in a family of three children. His sisters were "perfect." He was the "bad boy," the savage who had to be tamed, particularly in the eyes of his father, whose manner of handling and disciplining him was not to hit, but to mock and demean. The conjuring of the sense of shame in Kevin was a major method of control. Kevin had a vivid memory of when his father, in a shopping mall, tore a paper visor from his head and yelled that only stupid people wore those because they did not offer any protection for the top of the head, and that was what hats were for. Kevin's metaphor was frequently repeated when he complained about his own sons' mother letting them ride roughshod over her and how she let them dress in slovenly clothes so they looked shabby physically, making him look bad as a provider. Kevin was a strict man who loved his sons and did not tolerate these children being high spirited or teasing. When the police were dispatched to Kevin's house by his ex-wife for a "safety inspection," Kevin became extremely upset. This was how the loop went—from mother's invasive attacks when safety was at stake to father's temper tantrums about being treated without respect. When the metaphors were understood, they were explained simply to each parent. For instance, mother was told that father was particularly sensitive to respect and respectability. Knowing this, she had a choice. She could choose to upset him by being disrespectful or cast her requests in respectful terms, which would, in turn, help her get what she wanted. Gradually she was able to be nonprovocative because she was aware that otherwise she was not making her children safe, which both in fact and metaphorically was her primary focal issue.

Intrapsychic Issues

The final area to assess is the intrapsychic. Knowing the self-image, defensive structure, and vulnerabilities of an individual can help a PC make an appropriate plan. It is here that an inventory of losses a person has experienced is taken. An awareness of the client's loss history and the resulting present anxieties and vulnerabilities will greatly aid in understanding that individual. It can be helpful to inquire as to the type and frequency of losses a person has experienced. For instance, if a client has had a succession of losses in which girlfriends have always been stolen away by a more talented or attractive male, one may immediately anticipate a strong reaction by that person to anyone who happens to wander into his ex-spouse's life. One would proceed cautiously, particularly initially, about including any new person to join into a three-way discussion that previously had been a two-way discussion about such issues as the upbringing of the children. Additionally, one would wish to know if there is any diagnosable *DSM-IV* condition. If there is a thought disorder present, arbitration rather than mediation may have to be a more frequently utilized intervention technique.

Furthermore, clients' strengths as well as their vulnerabilities need to be assessed. Often strengths are complimentary in a high-conflict couple. For example, a highly organized person may marry a person with more difficulty in terms of establishing focus. Knowing the strengths of a client may offer a base upon which to build structure in which each parent can best function.

INTERVIEWS

The most helpful assessment technique is likely to be the interview. Interviewing the couple together, if they will allow it, as to the nature of impasses they face is helpful and enlightening to the PC. Individual interviews serve to develop some sense, in addition, of each individual's past as well as the past marital experiences. Ultimately, the PC is searching for an overarching conceptualization of what is going on between the couple. Of particular interest is how each member of the couple triggers the other and escalates the conflict. Three areas for which interview information should be collected are the individual's vulnerabilities, his or her composite of injuries, and his or her track record in terms of coping with stress and difficult situations in the past (Garrity and Baris 1994).

PARENTS

A good history of the marriage and divorce can be helpful in assessing the current situation. Each parent will have a different version, and comparing those differences can shed much light on what is important to each parent and what wounds are being nursed. The more either client seems to be operating at the third level of narcissistic wounds, as discussed in Chapter 2, the higher the conflict is likely to be and the more difficult the interventions will be.

In interviews, there are some items to listen for as a client speaks of the divorce. The more of these that are present, the more difficult the task is likely to be and the more careful and deliberate the Parenting Coordinator must be in decision making.

1. *An absence of sadness about the divorce loss.* For most divorcing couples, there is sadness about the loss of the relationship, the impact on the children, and a general sense of having failed in some manner. Individuals who experience no sadness are sending a signal that they have been able to compartmentalize the marriage and the relationship it represented. The relationship has been drained of feeling, which implies it can be treated as an "it." By being an "it," it is not a part of them; therefore, those who populated the marriage (the spouse, the children, the in-laws) can be handled in a calculated, unfeeling manner. A lack of sadness is evidence of a lack

of acknowledgment of loss, as grieving is the way one lets go of the loss. If grief is not recognized, a person can remain at impasse in the divorce with no progress toward healing, with a tendency to re-experience old conflicts in the same ways.

2. *An inability to see anything positive in the other parent.* An inability to see anything positive in the other parent, especially when directly asked, indicates that the parent is being or has been *objectified,* in other words, stripped of all positive regard. Without positive emotional meaning, a person may be handled in any expeditious way that helps one reach one's goals. Turning the other parent into an emotionally harmful "thing" sets the stage for the improper drawing of boundaries described in Chapter 2. It is a sign of binary thinking—all good or all bad—a necessary requisite for brutality without conscience.

3. *Justification for the marriage in terms of victimization.* People with high-conflict potential will often position themselves as victims of pressures greater than themselves. For instance, a marriage will be justified in terms of an out-of-wedlock pregnancy in which the person "had to get married" to give the child a name. This signals a lack of responsibility for what happened, with the single exception that they were trying to do the right thing and became trapped because of their good intentions. They hold themselves blameless for the marital problems from the very beginning decision to marry.

4. *Speaking of the other parent in the third person.* A quick signal of depersonalization and thus objectification is to call one's ex-spouse "the mother" or "the father." The signal is that the former relationship is being laundered of affect, and, without affect, the person can be treated as an object and manipulated without feeling.

5. *"Jekyll and Hyde" statements about the other parent.* The client describes the other parent as a person with a dual

personality, as loving one moment and then turning into an abusive, predatory monster the next. What you must listen for is the extent to which the client polarizes the other parent, signaling binary thinking. The more the other parent can be compartmentalized into good and bad, the more easily they can be handled without feeling when they are in their "Hyde" mode. Normally one thinks of a person as having strengths and weaknesses, of presenting a continuum of personal functioning. The kind, loving person still exists in the same body as the angry person. In such a conceptualization, one is reassured that the loving person is still there and will again emerge. The binary approach, as is reflected in such "Jekyll and Hyde" thinking, removes one whole facet of a person, leaving only evil, which can then be fought without mercy.

6. *A strong feeling of never having been loved,* and,

7. *A feeling of abandonment or desertion in a situation many people would have left long ago.* Both positions 6 and 7 indicate a sense of innocence and victimization. One's self-image is cleansed by defining a heroic struggle, trying to be loved, that failed through no fault of the protagonist. There is a strong prevailing sense that the client felt entitled to something they did not know how to achieve. There will be many stories about efforts to please, all of which were rejected or failed. Such positions reflect the client's sense of narcissistic wound—an emotional hunger that was never fed. The power in the situation is projected onto the nongiving other, while the client paints a picture of sincere effort doomed to failure because of the unresponsiveness of the spouse.

8. *A strong tendency to project blame and to position oneself as blameless without a trace of ambivalence.* Often this comes in the form of the only mistake the client made was to trust the "wrong" person. The client positions himself/herself

as the victim of the wily ways of the ex-spouse. This can move into the "Jekyll and Hyde" position as well. The PC must look for the defense of *projection of blame.* It is important to recognize that a basic tenet in the projection of blame is that, because it is always the other person's fault, the client learns little from experience because he/she is always reacting to another's machinations. Such an attitude does not augur well for cure by psychotherapy because there is a resistance to insight, that is, the locus of control always lies outside of the client. Another variation on this theme is found when a client states: "If only he (she) would stop what he (she) is doing, then I could stop what I am doing." Control and responsibility are projected onto the other parent and the victimized parent remains blameless because he/she is merely reacting to incoming stimuli.

9. *"He (She) is no longer a member of our family."* It can be helpful to see the parent and the children separately and to pose questions that begin "Who in your family . . . ?" A red flag in this situation is a parent who will reprimand, even if gently, children for including the absent parent in the current family constellation. By age 10 or so, most children are enough aware of the family party line not to bring up the absent parent. Young children, however, will often chatter away happily about activities with the absent parent. When the parent present in the interview moves to exclude the absent parent from the children's configurations of their family, a boundary is crossed. Husbands and wives divorce, but children do not divorce their parents. Easing the other parent out of the children's notion of family signals a lack of boundary between the parent and the children and can serve as a red flag toward the beginning of alienation or of the reshaping of reality.

10. *A history of professional shopping.* In extreme cases, the

parent can signal polarized thinking by moving from professional to professional until someone is found who agrees and remains in agreement with that parent's version of reality. A variation on this is the lawyer who overidentifies with his client, or the therapist who vigorously defends a client as if they had heard the whole story rather than just one side of the story. A common path taken is that of shopping many pediatricians until a parent finds one who will support the notion of sexual abuse. This symptom is extreme and obvious, but does signal great high-conflict potential.

11. *The presence of a perpetually dumbfounded parent.* In our experience, the most common pattern for high-conflict couples is that both parents have a role in sustaining the conflict. Sometimes one parent seems helpless in countering the angry parent's acting out. Because of their passivity and inability to mount an effective defense, these parents continuously reinforce the acting out because they continually give ground. Often such individuals will attempt to surround themselves with experts who will fight back for them. With the "dumbfounded parent" there is usually a background history of conflict avoidance and early experiences with degrading parents.

12. *A record of significant lawyer contact over inconsequential issues.* Corollaries of this can include no conversations between attorneys, only court actions. If a PC gets the impression that each client is paying a lawyer to simply fight with the other party's lawyer, high conflict has long been present. High-conflict couples create a climate of rage. It is difficult for the unsuspecting professional not to be swept up in the rage. Keeping your temper and sense of perspective is difficult in a highly seductive environment that begs for the union of individual anger into a more powerful joint rage. In this instance, one is reminded of an old joke about people beginning to look

like their dogs after living with them for ten years. Often attorney behavior, or a strong polarization between other professionals, such as mother's therapist and father's attorney, or the guardian *ad litem* and the children's therapists, signal the seductive power of anger and the operation of a polarizing narcissistic rage. An example is the one in which each time a high-conflict parent reached a mediated settlement over an issue, the other parent's lawyer would call the PC and say something to the effect of "my client will sign this only if you get his ex to agree to two extra days of parenting time a month." Here, the attorney resisted letting go of his advocacy function and saw each agreement as leverage for furthering his client's agenda. The PC needed several in-person conferences with the attorney to explain the parenting coordination process and how it differed from one-sided advocacy.

Our experience indicates that clients tend to talk within the framework of a metaphor. Simply, a metaphor is something (*A*) that serves as a symbol of something else (*B*). Therefore, whenever one speaks of *A*, *B* is also being talked about. One of the first tasks of the PC is to "pierce" the metaphor so as to understand the underlying issues that are being addressed and to enter the metaphor and to promote healing.

For example, Deborah, Kevin's ex-wife and the mother of twin sons, frequently called the police when she could not reach her sons by telephone when they were visiting their father. In the summer, Kevin and the sons were often in the yard and did not hear the telephone. A police car would swoop in and take the boys and their father by surprise, to say nothing of sending a tremor of alarm throughout the neighborhood. If one of the sons called Deborah while he was angry at his father, he could create an immediate uproar by telling his mother that his father was being mean to him. A visit by the police was an immediate consequence of such a call. In this case, the child could act out with relative impunity because "that crazy mother of mine" called the police, so it was the mother, not the child, who was responsible for the pandemonium. In essence, anything that appeared to threaten the safety of her children prompted Deborah to immediately call the authorities to investigate and protect. There had also been, in the context of this pattern, several calls to Social Services over possible abuse issues.

Deborah's childhood had been a difficult one. She was raised in a rural area as an only child. He father was psychotic, but his illness could be controlled by medication. As often happens, as his medication brought him to even functioning he would feel "cured" and stop taking it without telling anyone. He was then subject to violent psychotic episodes during which family members were assaulted. Being in a rural area made a rapid response by officials difficult, and Deborah's mother's general passivity and ability to suffer abuse often meant that the isolated family dealt with their own problems, often by simply covering up. During her own marriage, Deborah stated that her husband, Kevin, did not earn much money, so they had to live on what she considered the wrong side of town. His job took him away for protracted periods of time, so she felt abandoned in an unsafe neighborhood. Here a PC can sense echoes from the mother's childhood, in which she was abandoned by a passive mother to an unsafe father. Deborah's metaphor was *safety*. When she talked about her sons, she was constantly mentioning issues of their safety and her continuing worries when they were out of her sight. Her way of handling safety issues was to call in an authority, whom she felt had more power and could "make" her husband behave—something she could not do to her father when she was a child. Simply, when she spoke of her children's safety, she was also talking about her own profound sense of vulnerability around men she loved—her father and her ex-husband. There was a blurred boundary between her legitimately frightening experience as a child and her view of what was happening to her children. She could not discriminate between her childhood and that of her children. In rescuing them, she also rescued herself and "undid" what had happened to her. This time, she did not have to be passive and rely on others; she could take action herself.

Understanding the mother's metaphor provided a conduit through which the PC could speak in terms the mother could hear. By talking with her about safety and couching decisions in terms of safety, the PC could engage her defenses and have them work for the solution, rather than work to create uproar. For instance, it was pointed out to her that calling the police was actually unsafe because of the harm they might accidentally inflict if they mistook the situation, and the harm to her boys in terms of their neighborhood reputation. Wherever possible, interventions were always phrased in terms of their intent to create a safe environment for the children. Dissonance was set up within her about Kevin's lack of safe behavior and her own unsafe response. So, knowing the metaphor, the PC could co-opt the destructive side of her acting out by asking her to behave safely with her children rather than just sending someone to rescue them. The father's metaphor was *respect*. By calling the police, she showed him no respect, which escalated his responses to her.

An evaluation of the metaphors the client uses to couch complaints about the other parent is essential. When the PC understands the metaphor, the PC may cast communications into the metaphor as well and touch a particularly resonant spot in the client. This may elicit cooperation. For instance, if a mother constantly talks about how unsafe the children are with the father and casts a majority of her objections to the father having access to the children because of the lack of safety in his behavior, there is a medium in which to communicate. The more you can speak to solving safety issues with that parent, the greater the likelihood of acceptance of decisions.

The father, on the other hand, was directly informed that the mother's main issue was safety. If he wanted to quell the fighting, it was important to observe safety precautions and speak to his ex-wife in these terms about issues. If he wanted to upset her, by all means he could do something that appeared unsafe with the children, but he would likely experience as much pain as she when the police arrived at his door. The use of "safety" as the medium of communication with the mother worked. The impact was gradual, but over six months much of the mother's acting out calmed and diminished because she heard, without having to ask, that safety was of concern to the PC as well as to the father. By telling the father he had a choice, to either speak to safety and have a calm existence or be purposely unsafe and provoke the mother, the issue was addressed. Of course, she would have over-responded to a provocation and his life with the children would have been more difficult, but sometimes a jab is irresistible, regardless of the consequences. The father saw this as a choice he had, once he understood that safety was the metaphor in which all communication with mother needed to take place. Choosing safety and not provoking gave him a great feeling of superiority and power because he saw the issue of safety as an irrational belief that mother held and thus he could be more mature and more adult by humoring her "childish" worry. He then added to his "respect" for himself.

In this example lies the essence of being a good Parenting Coordinator. The conflict stopped (on this issue at least). It was not a therapist's solution in which a parent obtained self-insight into a distortion of reality. Instead, the distortion was accepted as a constant and then a method was put in place to cope with it. The issue was not how to rid the mother of her obsession with safety but, rather, how to deal with her obsession in such a way as to manage it and control it. In our experience, this is one of the most difficult lessons for a professional to learn: One *manages* the symptom, one does not *cure* or erase the symptom.

A knowledge of the defenses and of the metaphors into which a warring parent's irrationalities are poured are essential for case management. Conversations with a client must always acknowledge his or her individual issues. The issues will frequently be overdetermined, as in the example of the safety-obsessed mother. Her safety issues had roots that were once reality based in the out-of-control behavior of a psychotic father. Now, because of being "abandoned" and left unsafe by him, her perception of the world as a dangerous place became the defining issue in the high conflict with the father. In this mother's mind not only was she protecting her children, she was also undoing her own childhood in protecting them, as she had been left unprotected by an inadequate mother. The boundary between this mother and her children was very faint. Her distortion was, "I lived a dangerous childhood, therefore you also live a dangerous childhood." Communicating within, and soothing the fears caused by, that distortion greatly diminished the interparental conflict. It is an effective technique, but requires that a PC first understand and then pierce the metaphor within which high-conflict communication takes place. In assessing the metaphor, one understands how communications must be couched so as to be heard and have an effect.

FORMS OF ASSESSMENT

Decide what kind of assessment, if any, will be performed prior to intervention in the family. An assessment may take many different forms, such as:

- a review of previous evaluations (i.e., custody evaluations, psychological evaluations, treatment reports, etc.)
- information gathered from other professionals currently active with the family, such as attorneys, therapists, school personnel, child-care providers, and others
- an assessment of the children including their psychological functioning and developmental levels and how the parental conflict is affecting them
- an assessment of the parents, individually and in interac-

tion with one another, to determine parenting strengths and weaknesses

- an assessment of the impasse between the parents in order to understand the cause for the ongoing high conflict, including the contribution of others, such as extended family members and/or other professionals involved with the family. *In the Name of the Child* (Johnston and Roseby 1997) has an excellent protocol for assessing the impact of high conflict on the children.

Frequently a PC does an assessment that includes several of the areas mentioned above. It is important to be clear with the parents in the initial meetings as to what, if any, assessment will be done and what issues can be addressed before the assessment is complete. It is wise to consider delaying any interventions until after the assessment phase even if the parents present an emergency. Remember that these parents have handled situations in some way prior to coming to a PC. They can be told that they will have to continue to use whatever methods or persons they have been using until the assessment phase is over.

Following the assessment phase, the PC may want to have an interpretive session to discuss his/her understanding. This time can be used to present a perspective of the family's dilemma in such a way that the parents can concur yet begin to see how their own actions have positive or negative effects on the children. A well-done interpretive session forms the foundation of a good working alliance with the parents as well as a reference point for later work.

CHILDREN

As important as the assessment of the adult impasses is, an assessment of the children's functioning and safety is also critical. The most powerful tool a PC has in working with a high-conflict couple is knowledge of the children and an ability to convey to the parents that it is for the children's benefit that the entire parent-coordination effort is mounted.

A PC should always meet with the children or receive input from a therapist who knows the children well and meets with them on an ongoing basis. There needs to be clarity, however, that a PC is not the children's therapist. It is of great comfort and adds much credibility if you can demonstrate that you know, for example, what a parent is talking about when he refers to child A's habit of scrunching up his nose when he smiles. At the same time, you must be very careful not to do to the children what the parents do, that is, put the children in the middle by asking questions that draw up conflicting loyalties. One of the authors, in the early and naive stages of his learning to be a PC, decided to ask a 9-year-old boy which school he wanted to attend. His mother had announced 10 days before school started that she was moving and placing the boy in a new school. He had been at his previous school since he was 6 years old. Naturally, the father had strenuously objected, particularly since the parents had joint custody. The mother had brought the boy to the session, and when he was asked where he wanted to go to school (although not in the mother's presence), he said he did not care, he wanted it to be an adult decision. He later left with his mother, but he returned with her in less than two minutes, in tears, saying that he really wanted to go to the school near his mother's house. The mother stoutly denied she had said anything to him, and she was probably telling the truth. We suspect he told her what he had said to the PC, and all it took was a look from the mother to send him into backfiring because he did not want to hurt her feelings. The PC must be very careful about what children are asked.

Each PC will have his/her own preferred ways of understanding children, and those should be used to frame all PC actions. The royal route to parent cooperation is a conviction that the proposed solution to an impasse will be in their children's best interests. The children should be seen before parenting coordination functions begin, so that the parents know the PC is aware of the children's issues and position in the family and, most important, that the PC has some sense of what kind of decisions will best work for the children.

Arenas to be explored are:

- the general functioning level for each child
- the coping mechanisms each child employs to deal with parental conflict
- the kind of alignment each child has with each parent and any other key players in the family drama
- the normal developmental issues and tasks each child faces
- issues surrounding each child's safety
- medical issues that may influence decisions about each child's care

If a custody evaluation exists, it can often be of enormous help in answering the above questions. The PC will have to decide what information is most helpful to function in the children's best interests. The issue is not to spend enormous sums of money on a full diagnostic workup of the children but, rather, to have a strong sense of each child's needs. That knowledge is then used to present a credible picture to the parents that says, "I know your child and we can share our knowledge of her strengths and weaknesses." As we have stated repeatedly, a PC's knowledge base of the children is the basis for cementing a working relationship with each parent.

We strongly recommend that PCs interview the children's external caretakers and teachers. PCs have to be careful to assess if the external person is aligned with one parent or the other, but the information such individuals possess about the children's functioning outside of the immediate family can serve as a baseline for comparison with what the parents say about the children's functioning. We recommend that PCs be very cautious if not reluctant in asking the children what they want in an impasse situation because children tend to hear the question as "Whom do you love the most?"

Questions regarding the children for which a PC should have working answers before beginning to help solve impasses are:

- What has been the impact of the conflict on the children?
- How have the children learned to cope with the conflict?
- Is there any area in which the children are not safe in the conflict?
- Given the current state of the children's needs, what principles need to guide my decisions?

Psychological testing may be used. The Rorschach, in particular, can be a rich trove of information about how a parent processes the world. Early Rorschach work in this area seems to indicate that high-conflict couples have extremely unique ways of looking at the world, quite different than those of run-of-the-mill clients. Their organization can also be quite chaotic. A parent's processing style can impact the children. The use of testing should be an individual choice. Further, test results should be used to augment impressions from clinical interviews and collateral reports. Tests should never be used as a substitute for hands-on, face-to-face investigation.

5

Education

Educating parents is one of the less stressful and more enjoyable arenas a Parenting Coordinator (PC) functions within. While most states require parent education classes, these are designed for the low-conflict parents of divorce. Parents have typically attended these classes early in the divorce process when many issues may have taken precedence over the well-being of their children. Often the educative function can be woven in with the other PC functions, providing some welcome respite from the difficult topics. Education can also be an opportunity to lay the groundwork for difficult decisions the PC can foresee. Parents can be provided with small amounts of information as they are ready to assimilate it, thus enlarging their capacity to look at issues in a larger framework later down the road. The primary issues for which increased knowledge will benefit parents include:

1. Child development, especially the tasks their children will be focused on given their ages. First parents need to

understand the normal emotional issues for children of different ages and then the manner in which these issues may be disrupted because of the divorce process.

2. The mechanics of parenting alone as a single parent and of co-parenting in a civil manner with someone who may now trigger profound feelings of anger, hurt, and/or distrust.

3. Conflict resolution. This will involve theory, rationale, and most important, skills and techniques.

4. An understanding of legal terms, the legal system, and the process of preparing for and possibly going to court.

5. Family issues. This can cover a large range of issues from involvement of grandparents and other relatives, significant others or stepparents, blended families, dating, and for all parents of divorce, redefining a sense of identity as a family unit.

6. Resources for specific problems. High-conflict families can pose unique challenges to the PC. Conflict may arise over issues such as private versus public education for the children, special needs of one or more of the children, medical concerns, religious decisions, or permission for specific activities. The PC may need to first seek education in a specific area in order to advise the parents regarding their children.

CHILD DEVELOPMENT
AND NEEDS OF THE CHILDREN

Parents must be educated about what is in their children's best interests to shift their perspective from what is not in the parents' best interests. Children who are not exposed to high degrees of conflict over long periods of time have the best prospects for continuing their own development in a healthy fashion and growing into responsible adults capable of forming their own intimate relationships. One of the primary tasks of a PC may be to help the parents devise or modify their time-sharing plan. High-conflict parents require a unique plan tailor-made for their family, which will minimize the children's exposure to the conflict. "One size fits all" does not work for conflicted parents. Thus, the PC must be well versed in child development theory and should be able to help the parents understand their children's needs at various stages of development. A Parenting Coordinator must be creative in finding ways to maximize the time with each parent according to the emotional readiness of each child, while protecting the child from exposure to conflict. A PC can educate the parents about the needs of the children, given their ages, as separate from the needs of the parent. Parents have a tendency to take time sharing very personally, to look at their own needs, and to forget about the needs of their children. Wallerstein and Lewis (1998), who followed children of divorce over a twenty-five-year period, found that inflexibly imposed court-ordered visitation failed miserably in building healthy, respectful parent–child relationships: "No single child who saw his or her father under a rigidly enforced court order or unmodified parental agreement had a good relationship with him after reaching adulthood" (p. 376). Several areas of particular difficulty for high-conflict parents, which emphasize the need for focus by the parents with the help of the PC on the children's developmental stages, are discussed next.

Transitions

The customary guidelines used to develop time-sharing plans along developmental lines can be a starting point, but most high-conflict parents cannot transition their children on a frequent basis without difficulty. One key factor in successful transitions is to foster the disengagement of the parents from each other. Transitioning the children in some fashion that does not allow the parents to have an opportunity to have contact or communication is the goal. This can take many shapes or forms: transitioning by pick up or delivery at the school or daycare provider's home, transitioning through a neutral location or supervised center, or allowing the children to walk in or out of each home to the waiting car of the other parent. Obviously, the older the child, the easier the planning will be for drop-off and pick-up. Very creative thinking will be required for the infant and toddler. Keeping in mind the necessity for no contact between the high-conflict parents, the blocks of parenting time might need to be designed according to the available transition points rather than according to the ideal developmental model. For example, a child who might customarily have a weekend visitation from Friday to Sunday evening may need to extend the visitation time to Monday morning so that drop-off can be at the school rather than at the other parent's home on Sunday evening. The stress to the child of adding on an additional overnight will have to be weighed against the stress of experiencing arguing, denigration, and possibly physical confrontations between the two parents. Typically, longer blocks of parenting time and fewer transitions work best to avoid exposure of the children to parental conflict. Chapter 10 presents a sample parenting plan for high-conflict parents with school-aged children.

Children of Different Ages

The PC can educate the parents about clever extra arrangements that maximize time with both parents. For example, children of different ages might benefit from different blocks of time with the parents. It is not necessary for all of the children to visit together at all times. Very young children might be returned to the primary caretaking parent while the older children stay on for an extended visitation time. Often children of different genders appreciate and, in fact, look forward to an evening alone with each parent. The PC can assist the parents in planning special time for these parenting time periods that maximize skill building and activities that one child might thoroughly enjoy and the other finds no pleasure in at all. For example, one child might adore learning a physical skill or sports-related activity whereas another is more artistic. Each child can have the opportunity to pursue a desired activity with a parent during an alone visitation time.

Adolescents

Adolescents pose their own challenges to parents and PCs alike. A teenager, in all honesty, may not have a great deal of desire to spend long periods of time with either parent. Sometimes the non-residential parent takes this personally, and yet it is a very normal and expected developmental stage for an adolescent to prefer to spend weekends with friends rather than with either parent. Other adolescents will be interested and able to move between living at two homes if each parent is willing to support them in their community activities, is agreeable to friends coming over, and, of course, is a ready chauffeur until driving privileges are earned. The PC can educate the parents about these adolescent needs in general as well as the specific needs of their children.

Holidays

Holidays may need to be reconceptualized following divorce. Maintaining old traditions can be difficult, and, most of all, painful. Finding new and creative ways to celebrate and share the significant holidays can be offered by the PC. Children should be able to enjoy the holidays with their parents rather than being stressed out by the conflict that may surround holiday arrangements. The PC can talk to the parents about holiday arrangements that other parents have found to be successful and that minimize the strain on the children.

Children as Individuals

The PC is an advocate for the children, not as a therapist but as an ally assisting the children to have the best relationship possible with each parent by having the children's needs and wishes respected. A PC should have the right to access and gather information about the children, such as about their current functioning, needs, wishes, and patterns of attachment. This information can then be communicated to the parents to help guide their decisions. Parents, in essence, are educated by the PC as to who their children are and how their children see and experience the world. Very often, the children seen in the parenting coordination process are the ones whose parents present opposing viewpoints about the wishes of the children. This conflict can be clarified by the PC getting to know the children individually and as a sibling group as well as by talking with any significant professionals involved with their children. If any of the children have a therapist, often the PC can be the communication link between the therapist and the parents, relieving the therapist from the awkward position of being asked to make decisions for the parents. In this way, neither parent ends up angry at the therapist, as the anger can be directed at the PC, protecting the important supportive role the therapist has for the child experiencing the divorce conflict. The PC can then educate the parents about the children's needs, wishes, and feelings as separate from those of either parent. This is very critical, as many children caught in high-conflict divorces lose their voices. Currently, "whether the proceeding is a mediation or a judicial hearing, the focus is too often on the rights of the adults rather than on those of the child" (Mason 1999, p. 66). These children sacrifice their own individual opinions, wishes, and desires in order to please each parent. Over time, these children lose all sense of individuality and grow up very limited in their capacity to function in the adult world. The PC can play an extraordinarily important preventive role by being the voice of the children until such time as the children become strong enough to communicate for themselves.

Educating the Children

Educating the children directly is yet another unique role the PC may play. Children can be taught specific resources or strategies to use when caught between their arguing parents. Just as one parent might be educated as to the triggers of an anger-prone, demonstrative ex-spouse, the children can also learn to identify the triggers of an angry parent and to avoid becoming a victim of that parent's rage. Older children can often handle semi-endangering situations with the proper education. Recognizing the signs of a parent who has been drinking may be taught as well. A plan can then be created with somewhat older children for what they will do if the problem begins during a visit or at the pick-up time. The PC can assist children in developing and practicing a safety plan.

The PC is a professional who can be there for the family over time. This is critically important, as the children are not stagnant; they continue to grow emotionally and to shift the demands they place on their parents. What might work for a preschooler will no longer work for a school-aged child with homework and after-school activities. The PC can educate and reinforce his/her knowledge about children's changing needs over time, and can advise parents about what suits each child best at any given age.

COMMUNICATION SKILLS AND CO-PARENTING

Most high-conflict parents have a profound inability to communicate and problem solve together without blaming, abusing verbally, becoming volatile and angry, and possibly being physically aggressive. Some high-conflict parents are capable of curbing these impulses, appreciating their negative impact on the children, and demonstrate the maturity to learn and practice new conflict-resolution styles. Other high-conflict parents simply refuse to believe their style is any part of the problem. These parents show little empathy for the impact their behavior has on their children. Frequently, entrenched parents have a history of volatility and impulse-discharge problems and enjoy the sense of empowerment they experience from creating fear and intimidation in others. When aggression has been a primary problem-solving style throughout life, the likelihood of change is minimal. The PC, therefore, must access the capacity for change and for learning new strategies. The research is clear in this area. If a parent cannot contain his or her anger, both the children and the other parent must be protected from exposure to it. A PC must initially think through which pathway will result in the most beneficial outcome for the children: teaching the parents communication and problem-solving skills or establishing complete disengagement such that there is no avenue for communication and problem solving other than through the PC. It is helpful for all parents to understand that divorcing couples need to go through a period of disengagement if there has been high conflict. Some will establish a basis, over time, to move toward more cooperative co-parenting; others will never establish this basis and will need to remain disengaged until the children are old enough to emancipate and develop separate relationships with each parent as they wish.

CONFLICT RESOLUTION TECHNIQUES

The PC will draw on conflict resolution ideas repeatedly. Techniques for containment of anger can be taught. High-conflict parents may be very reactive. Allowing twenty-four or forty-eight hours before responding to a communication that is not truly an emergency can often result in a calmer, more thoughtful reaction. Transitioning of the children is a time that rekindles old animosities. Parents can be taught techniques for remaining calm, focused on the task at hand, and unresponsive to the "baiting" of the other parent. Some parents are capable and interested in their own growth; these parents will readily accept help in identifying triggers for arguments and how to avoid them. A parent might need a way to save face, avoid, or self-soothe when confronted by the angry outbursts of the ex-spouse. These can be developed, practiced, and refined with the assistance of the PC. Just knowing the PC is in place comforts many parents, as an objective third party is looking on and available to intervene if need be. Individuals with impulse-control problems tend to act out the most when no one else except the ex-spouse is around to hear or see them. Awareness that the out-of-control behavior might be reported to the PC by the other parent or the children creates a climate of possible exposure and also may serve as needed external control.

THE COURT AND THE LEGAL SYSTEM

PCs serve a very important educative function in helping parents understand the court and legal system. Often the PC can help an easily victimized or very upset parent to understand and use other creative problem-solving ideas that keep certain issues out of the legal system. Motions that are filed in divorce litigation are one-sided, framing an issue in a manner that benefits the attorney's client. Explaining this to both parents can often help keep issues in their proper perspective. Some PCs are even successful at bringing some of these issues to resolution, saving the parents the time, expense, and hurt of courtroom proceedings.

Occasionally a high-conflict family will have so many professionals involved that confusion is bound to result. A PC might be able to coordinate the input of the different professionals, easing the complexities of too many voices and differing opinions. A PC might also educate each parent as to the role each professional assumes or cannot assume. In many states, for example, a Guardian *ad litem* (GAL) may be appointed for the children. Most parents do not understand the role of a GAL and whether he or she has decision-making power, confidentiality, and respect within the courtroom. Many parents have the roles of mental health professionals confused. Therapists are not the same as custody evaluators. It is a conflict of roles, typically, for a therapist to give court testimony regarding an opinion about custody. A therapist has confidentiality, with a few exceptions, whereas an evaluator has been agreed upon or court appointed and has no confidentiality. Any information revealed to an evaluator may be admitted into the courtroom. Yet both a therapist and an evaluator may be of the same profession; both may be psychologists, social workers, or psychiatrists. It is understandable that this is confusing.

Legal terms are not part of most individuals' vocabulary until they find themselves in the process of a divorce proceeding. Suddenly words such as "joint custody" or "joint legal custody" or "residential custody" get bantered about. Most parents need repeated explanations of the term "joint custody" and the distinction between residential and legal custody.

PCs who have no legal background must educate themselves prior to assuming the important role of educating divorced or divorcing parents. High-conflict parents tend to distort information provided to them. It is thus critical that the PC be well versed in issues, especially legal issues, which will be addressed in the process of working with the parents. At a minimum, a PC must thoroughly understand the standards for custody determinations, visitation, endangerment, and relocation. Even the language used to discuss these issues can trigger reactive parents. The term "living arrangements" is often preferable to the term "custody," and "time sharing" or "parenting time" is a kinder term to many parents than "visitation." Understanding the major decisions that must be finalized into a legal co-parenting plan is mandatory for every PC.

The educative role, obviously, needs to be uniquely tailored to the divorce situation, safety concerns, and ages of the children. The well-being of children can be assured by an attentive PC in a way that is not possible for a therapist, GAL, or attorney.

The PC has thus been developed as an interdisciplinary professional: a person who provides a communication link, fosters relationship building, represents the needs of the children, contains the destructive conflict, and eases family members into a healthier, more civilized post-divorce adjustment. In each of these areas, the PC educates the parents and children in avenues that will direct them toward growth and a resumption of "normal" functioning.

FAMILY ISSUES

One function that the Parenting Coordinator might assume is that of teaching parents about developmentally appropriate parent–child interactions. Some of this might include teaching projective play techniques to parents of younger children, such as using open-ended projective drawings like family drawing, drawing fantasies, or wish fulfillment. In addition, parents might be able to play with action figures with their children or even in sand trays and elicit a great deal of emotional material. Parents might be taught that children's play is metaphorical and that often children will express their emotional issues through expressive media. Some parents need to be taught that it is appropriate to sit down on the floor and play with children in ways that build communication and rapport in general. Many parents will benefit as well from a discussion of what is developmentally appropriate for children. It helps if parents understand when children may be best taught to read, what their cognition and ability to conceptualize will be at different stages, and thus, some appropriate activities, both intellectual and physical or athletic might be explored. It is most helpful, of course, that parents understand the fact that pre-adolescents and adolescents become increasingly involved with reference to their peers and that they need to be able to stay in touch with their peer group to build a sense of their own identity. Children at the stage of pre-adolescence and early adolescence often need to build their sense of identity vis-à-vis who they can identify with, that is, which of their friends they feel that they are just like, and which of their peers they feel they are very different from and in what respects. Children of this age frequently are in telephone contact with their friends and enjoy planning activities with their parents to include their friends.

The PC can often encourage relationships with distant parents as well. Teaching resources for maintaining long-distance relationships may be an important function of the PC. This would extend to teaching the concepts of structuring telephone calls, perhaps subscribing to the same newspapers or reading the same magazines, or watching the same sporting events on TV and being able to discuss them. The parents might be taught that they may continue their relationship with that child at a geographical distance by leading into the strengths that the parent has to offer the child, such as math tutoring or story reading. All of these things can take place over the telephone or through email.

The PC can help parents to teach children that the children need to be able to distinguish their own independent relationships with their parents and extended family of their parents from that of the relationship the parents might have with each other. It can be most helpful for the parents to say, "Yes, it is clear that I don't get along with your father [or mother], but I certainly expect you to maintain a loving and respectful relationship with your father [or mother] and with your grandparents, aunts, uncles, and cousins on his [her] side of the family as well."

Moreover, it is important that parents and children try to work on a "consensus model" of communication whereby parents will listen to their children and will consider heavily their input, while the parents still maintain decision-making authority. If children recognize that they have had input into the formulation of a given decision, they can more easily endorse the decision and live by it in terms of the rules or resolutions for their behavior that may be implied or stated in any given decision.

RESOURCES

Sometimes parents and children are in need of educational or other outside resources to help them to enhance their parenting or relationship experience. This may fall into the purview of the PC as well. For example, the PC may share knowledge of existing summer or community workshops or resources to which the parent and child may subscribe together and be involved in together. Or it may involve referrals to therapists for the child, for the parent, or a therapist to help strengthen the relationship between the parent and the child. It may involve referrals to educational programs or educational assessments if the child is having difficulty. There may be referrals to volunteer programs or activities that the parent and child might participate in together or that either one of them might enjoy participating in alone. It is helpful if the PC has a good general knowledge base of the resources in the community in which the parents or children are living.

6

Interfacing

One of the most important functions a Parenting Coordinator (PC) performs is that of a communication link between the various segments of the entire system involved with the high-conflict family. This includes aiding communication between the warring parents; between each parent and the children; and among all the various legal, mental health, medical, and educational professionals who may be involved with the family. Each case will require a different and unique combination of interface activities, but much of the PC's work falls in this broad category.

FAMILY

For a family embroiled in high conflict, a PC can be a neutral buffer for communication between parents who have difficulty talking with one another without escalating into shouting matches, name calling, or, worst of all, even violence. Children of high-conflict families often cite their parents' inability to get along and to talk in a civil manner with one another as the one thing they would most like changed. A PC can coach each parent in more effective and respectful ways to phrase requests or statements that might stir up conflict. The PC's growing knowledge of each parent's individual psychodynamics and the interactional dynamics between them is put to good use in this context. Over time, some couples slowly adopt more healthy and successful ways of communicating and resolving conflict. There are parents who, even with much help, cannot or will not change their ways; these couples need the PC to act as an intermediary, actually receiving messages from one parent, perhaps neutralizing the content, and then communicating the messages to the other. In this situation, the PC can neutralize messages that might inflame, and can assist in the task of focusing on the important information to be communicated or decisions to be made rather than on the frequently affectively charged tone of the message. These families often experience a lessening of the conflict because the opportunities for conflict are reduced. Their children then report feeling relieved and less stressed because their parents are fighting less.

There are other family members with whom the PC may wish to work. Stepparents are often critical people either in the maintenance of conflict or in its de-escalation. The Parenting Coordinator needs to know how a stepparent affects the situation and how best to involve, or not involve, them in the work of conflict resolution.

Extended family members are often key figures in the drama of high-conflict family life. It is not at all uncommon for a parent or sibling of one of the parents, in addition to a new step-parent or long-standing best friend, to fuel that parent's negative view of the ex-spouse and thus undermine efforts to modulate that parent's unrealistic demonizing of the other parent. On the other hand, extended family members can provide a haven for the children and may help soften a parent's rigid view of things. Again, the PC must assess the situation and decide how best to work with, and involve or to work around, such family and network members. Sometimes the work is directly with the other family members; sometimes it entails indirectly working with their influence on the larger system.

SYSTEMS AND PROFESSIONALS

Because high conflict often occurs in families whose members have significant emotional disturbances, and because high conflict itself hurts children (and prolongs conflict among adults), there are often a number of professionals already working with the family. However, the professionals may not know of each other's existence, much less confer on any regular basis. Sometimes the most valuable intervention a PC can effect is to change this situation. This may take the form of facilitating communication between or among the existing professionals, or it may involve more active intervention in the larger network with a goal of changing some aspects of the larger system's functioning. Some have called this case management or case coordination. A PC is often in a unique position to effectuate a case conference, or facilitate communication through other means, where professionals can confer with one another. Frequently, plans can then be made that benefit the children and the family. For instance, once school personnel are informed by the PC about the nature of the conflict between the parents, they can design strategies to help insulate the children from the damaging effects of parental conflict. This might include insuring that each parent is sent copies of important notices of events or is given a separate teacher conference time.

Mental Health

Through contact with the PC, individual psychotherapists for each parent might gain a new and more realistic understanding of the other parent. Often a parent's individual psychotherapist has only that parent's view of the ex-spouse and the children and has little opportunity to hear information that might modify or expand that view. It can be enormously helpful to a psychotherapist to hear the broad perspective because this may well shed light on the patient's way of processing information, including to what degree reality may be distorted. In this way, the PC is often in a unique position to offer a fuller view of the parents and their situation to professionals who have had contact with only one family member. In turn, it is very helpful for the PC to hear from a parent's therapist about that parent's individual dynamics and progress in psychotherapy. This can provide the PC with valuable clues about how best to work with that parent, especially in regard to what aspects of the parent's functioning might be confronted or changed and what might need to be worked around.

Psychotherapists for the children not only provide the children with help in managing the sequelae of their parents' divorce, they can also be an invaluable aid to the PC. Often the PC knows the children largely through contact with their psychotherapist rather than from direct contact. This manner of shielding the children from having to form yet another relationship can be especially beneficial in those cases where the children have had to meet numerous other professionals, such as child custody evaluators, attorneys, GALs, and so forth. The children's therapist is a crucial informant about what the children experience in their relationships with their parents and what parental behaviors are harmful to them. A strong working relationship between the PC and the children's therapist(s) is extremely important to successful work in the children's behalf.

There are frequently other mental health professionals involved with a family, such as custody or other forensic evaluators, or special advocates. They can be sources of a wealth of information for the PC. If an evaluation is occurring concurrently with the parenting-coordination process, the Parenting Coordinator should be clear with the family about exactly what, if any, information will be given to the evaluators. There are advantages to sharing information as well as to keeping it confidential. The scope of confidentiality will depend on the particular conflict-resolution process in which the family is engaged with the PC and on state law. Sometimes a re-evaluation takes place after temporary recommendations have been in place for a period of time. In this instance, the PC can often provide valuable feedback to the evaluators regarding the family's progress in reducing conflict or handling it productively. Visitation specialists often work with the family to provide either supervised visits or exchanges. Collaboration and communication between the visitation specialist and the PC are important in monitoring how the parents are doing in relating to their children, how well they can protect their children from the conflicts between them, and how the children are faring.

Social Services

Frequently, high-conflict families have contact with social service or child protection agencies because of abuse or neglect or allegations of such. The PC must have accurate information about any past or present abuse or about the investigation of any allegations one parent has made against the other. The PC should obtain the necessary releases of information, preferably during the contracting phase, in order to speak freely with any social service personnel who are involved with the family. In addition, the PC may be required by local law to report suspected abuse during the process of working with a high-conflict family. If this is the case, it is best to have a clause explaining mandatory reporting in the original PC contract. The PC must then decide how and when to inform the parents of such a report to social services or the police. One critical factor in making these decisions is the safety of the children and the impact of the information on the conflict between the parents. How one words such a disclosure to the parents often makes an enormous difference.

Legal

A PC must work within the parameters of the state laws. Not only does the law differ from state to state, but even within states across counties and municipalities there may be tremendous variance. The broad range of judicial discretion in the area of family law and parental rights often has a dramatic impact on the outcome of cases that are tried with similar facts in the same county in the same state, but by different judges.

It is essential that a PC have a basic, general familiarity with the applicable family law. The attendance at continuing legal education classes held by local bar associations can provide essential information regarding the law. The framework within which a PC must work is governed by the law, and it is critical to be aware of, and work within, those boundaries.

A PC must also be familiar with the conventions and customs of a particular legal jurisdiction and of the community at large. This is particularly true if the PC is new to the community. The social norms of a local community often govern interpretations and implementation of the state law. A PC who has taken the time and made the effort necessary to become familiar with the general law and community standards will have a significant advantage in educating and communicating with legal professionals.

The education of the judiciary is often challenging. Family law cases, particularly in geographic areas that do not have a family court, are often the most despised and frustrating to a judge. These cases consume an extraordinary amount of judicial resources, and judges are often uncertain as to what is best for the children. Judges will often admit that complicated custody cases are frequently more difficult than criminal cases.

It is essential in the education of judges regarding parenting coordination to incorporate the following: (1) that a PC is permissible under the law; (2) that a PC can reduce crowded dockets and keep cases out of court; and (3) that the children will benefit.

The presentation of the concept of a PC may be most effectively conducted at judicial conferences or other programs that have judges in attendance. It is essential that there be recognition of the very fine line that a judge must walk in participating in community or professional presentations. Judges must maintain their neutrality and, depending upon the arena, may not be free to question or give opinions. Therefore, the manner in which the introduction of the PC concept is presented may have great significance as to whether the concept is accepted.

If the PC concept is being introduced to a judge for the first time in a trial or hearing, then a certain amount of education should be incorporated into the testimony. Also, an attorney in the case would be well advised to prepare, in advance, a trial brief (memorandum of law) that delineates the legal authority for a PC. This is particularly true in those jurisdictions that have strict limitations on a court's ability to delegate authority in custody matters.

The education of attorneys who practice family law is most easily conducted through local bar associations or other organized groups of attorneys who have domestic relations as a focus of their practice. Bear in mind that the messenger can make a critical difference. It is essential that the concept of a PC be introduced by experts for whom the local bar has respect. Attorneys, upon first learning about a PC, may have significant and difficult legal questions relating to the concept, and these questions must be appropriately answered. The PC must recognize that the attorneys have serious ethical, legal, and moral obligations to a client and cannot risk recommending a PC without full understanding of what it means.

It is essential in the education of attorneys to incorporate the following: (1) that a PC is permissible under the law; (2) that the attorney is not compromising his duties to a client; (3) that a PC can solve problems for a client that the legal system may have been unable to solve; and (4) that the children will benefit.

It is important to recognize that attorneys often have significant training in areas outside of the law and may have substantial information about the client and the family. It is important that the PC be open to this information and not discount the attorneys' input in this regard.

It is appropriate to educate the attorney about the role that he/she may be playing in the conflict between the parents. This must be done with finesse and should never be demeaning or critical to the attorney. In cases that have an extensive history, the attorney and client may have a long-standing relationship, and the education of an attorney must take place in a way that realigns the attorney to be part of a working retinue of professionals supporting the family.

It is critical that the roles of the parent's attorney and PC be carefully defined and agreed upon. It is detrimental to a family if there is confusion in regard to these roles. If the PC develops the support of a client's attorney, in most cases an important bridge to the client will have been created.

The children may have a Guardian *ad litem* whose role is to protect their best interests. The specific roles and functions of a GAL vary from state to state, and it is important to be familiar with a particular state's policies and practices. The roles of the GAL and the PC may overlap, so it is crucial for a PC to initially determine whether there is a GAL involved with the family and, if so, what decision-making authority the GAL has and how coordination should occur. If the PC has arbitration power, it is especially important to discuss with the GAL how the two functions will fit together in a way that benefits the family and does not overlap or leave gaps. It can be difficult if the particulars are not worked out in advance. If a conflict arises and the PC arbitrates it, the dissatisfied parent may well seek out the GAL to overturn the PC's efforts. It is essential that the PC seek the GAL's input prior to making an arbitration award. Time spent hammering out the details of what role the GAL will play and what role the PC will play is time well spent.

Other Systems Linkages

The PC might very well need to also be connected to the other professionals or parts of the service-providing community that are involved with the client and the client's family. If there is a teacher, counselor, school psychologist, or school social worker who is involved with the family or providing services to the family, coordination with that person might be helpful. Perhaps the family has been involved with law enforcement and a probation officer or parole officer may be assigned and involved with the family as well. It would be important to remain connected and to maintain communication links with such a professional under these circumstances. Health-care professionals may be included as well. If there are special needs children or adults in the family who are receiving services from physical therapists, cognitive therapists, occupational therapists, visiting nurses, or any other health-care related services where health-care professionals are playing a directly supportive role to a family member, they need to be included and involved. Perhaps religious professionals might be critical as well. In some instances, a priest, a pastor, a rabbi, or other minister may be extremely helpful in terms of being part of an individual's extended support network and may be someone critical in terms of helping to guide the decisions of the parents. Clergy might be important to include at times in mediation or consultation or just general coordination of services to families. The PC needs to be able to make an accurate determination as to how much these professionals are involved with families and how much to include them and coordinate with them in providing optimal services to the family.

7

Intervention

A Parenting Coordinator (PC) intervenes through the general attitude and manner of approach when working with the clients, and through specific intervention techniques employed during the process. It is important to recognize that "modeling" is a powerful technique for changing undesirable behavior. Usually an intervention is intended to create a shift in attitude. Although an intervention may be directly focused on reaching a decision by breaking an impasse, such as using mediation or arbitration, it is also accomplished by the PC reframing or modeling an attitude. For example, a problem can be conceptualized in a manner that attempts to avoid polarization and rigid adherence to one point of view. A skilled PC adopts a respectful approach that emphasizes the well-being of the children and civility in how individuals interact with one another, and focuses proactively on the future rather than on the past and ascribing blame. This is accomplished by reframing issues, building empathy, setting limits, and staying grounded in the process. All of these techniques are geared toward helping the parents to change their perspective on issues and pave the way for them subsequently to change their behaviors.

An intervention is not simply using a technique. It is rather a pervasive attitude toward problem solving. A PC attempts to constantly model problem-solving techniques that enhance communication and avoid polarization of attitudes. An intervention technique that is not embedded in an overarching attitude of rational problem solving will be much less likely to work than one that is. The problem is to convey a total approach, an altered way of thinking about the world.

A PC must always be willing to intervene between the parents on behalf of the children's needs. Interventions may be as numerous and creative as any PC's ability may provide.

The PC role is one that at times may resemble walking in a mine field. The realm of the PC is actively in the middle of the conflict between the parents for the hearts, minds, and residences of their children. To effectively intervene in such intense conflict, the PC needs to be knowledgeable about conflict-management theory, skills, and processes. A PC should be trained in mediation by experts who teach a model of conflict management that can be used to diagnose a conflict situation. Although conflict-management skills may be taught in the fields of social work, law, or psychology, the processes of mediation involve an outlook and approach that is different and extremely valuable.

Preparation for intervening in high-conflict parental disputes involves understanding what the PC brings to the dispute as well as understanding the dynamics between the parents. The PC must be alert to what issues may trigger over-reactions, defenses, and negative feelings because of the PC's own past experiences. Issues of parenting, divorce, children, and the legal system tend to bring up intense feelings in PCs because of their own life histories. It is important that the PC be confident in the expertise and motivation that he or she has for being involved, as high-conflict parents often attack the PC during the process. Self-doubt is normal, and a willingness to explore the PC's own motivations and actions in any intervention is crucial to effective, genuinely helpful work with parents. The PC may make mistakes and be able to admit them to parents; however, the PC should not immerse him/herself in self-recrimination and doubt that meaningful work, overall, is taking place. Checking in with the PC's own feelings and a support system of colleagues during work with the parents is essential to staying sane and on track.

CONFLICT MANAGEMENT SKILLS

Focus on Process Rather Than on Solutions

Effective conflict management begins with thinking about a process that handles a flow of problems rather than focusing on solving a particular dispute (Fisher et al. 1994). The goal of the Parenting Coordinator in managing the conflict between parents is to conceptualize and put into place a process that moves the family forward. Sometimes the Parenting Coordinator may be the only professional who has an understanding of the entire situation and, therefore, is called upon to maintain a vision for the family. Part of the role of a Parenting Coordinator is to design the process, through mediation and/or negotiation with the parents or by the PC's imposition of a solution, that will help move the parents to more peaceful and healthy parenting. The solution will be one that the PC envisions and is desired by the children and other professionals working with the family.

Reframe the Issues

Each parent has a particular point of view of the dispute, the children's needs, and his or her own behavior as well as that of the ex-spouse. The PC can reframe the dispute in language that is not inflammatory and allows solutions to be found (Gold 1992, p. 225). The goal is to use neutral language to remove bias, positions, and judgment, and to state the problem clearly and in a manner that favors neither of the parents (Moore 1996, p. 217). Reframing is an art that produces immediate results in dealing with high-conflict parents and in defusing and refocusing hostility. For example, after listening to a father attack a mother for alienating the children from him, the PC can reframe that issue as, "You very much value your relationship with your children and want to strengthen it." It turns the focus from blaming the other parent to a statement that can be discussed in terms of behaviors for improving the parent's relationship with the children. The PC reframes the issue from negative to neutral and from blaming to future desired behavior. This is a powerful perceptual shift for high-conflict parents.

Look beyond Positions to Interests

Once an issue has been reframed into neutral language, the PC can explore the parents' ideas about the issue. Each parent will have a desired solution to any situation. For example, the mom is upset because the dad has been thirty to forty-five minutes late picking up the children for each transfer for the past month. Prior to the dad's arrival at the mom's home to pick up the children, the mom has been spending the time castigating the dad, either to the children or silently in her thoughts, for his irresponsibility, tardiness, unreliability, and lack of consideration for her needs. The children become agitated, either by their mother's direct attacks upon their father or by observing her tense posture, distress, and mannerisms. They fear the argument they know is coming when their dad arrives. The dad comes to the door, the mom bursts forth with a flurry of negative and hostile statements, and the dad responds defensively with his own litany of the mom's faults about being compulsive, insensitive to the demands of commuting, and running him down in front of the children. The children are, once again, forced to observe their parents arguing in loud and abusive voices. The dad may even slam the door behind the children and speed off from the mom's house, tires screeching. The parenting time has started in an ugly and negative way, and everyone is upset. As the mother recounts her narrative of the father's lack of punctuality to the PC, she states that the only solution to the problem is that the dad should miss his parenting time if he is more than fifteen minutes late and that he should pay for a babysitter if one is needed to allow the mom to go about her business. This is her position, that is, her favored solution to the problem. At that moment, that may be the only solution that she sees because of her anger. The dad responds with his demand that the mom can drop off the children at his place of employment if she is so concerned about him being on time. That is his position.

Rather than concentrating on the positions and demands of each parent, the PC should use the mediation skill of looking for underlying interests or needs. In the previous situation, the mother has a need to be able to plan her time and follow through with her own time commitments with punctuality. She also has a need to be acknowledged for the importance of her own activities. The father has a need to be given leeway in his scheduling because of the unpredictability of his job and traffic. He also needs to feel in control of his parenting time with the children. The PC should ask, either to her-/himself or to the parents, "What does each parent really care about in this particular situation?" The answer will help shed light on what is important about the issue to each parent. The PC will then explore with the parents, probe for, and articulate the underlying needs of each parent in the situation. The negotiations can then be structured to allow for a process that meets both parents' interests. For example, the PC, after stating each parent's interests and receiving agreement from each parent that the PC has indeed stated the interests accurately, can reframe the issue as, "How can the mom's need to be on time for her commitments be met while also allowing the dad some flexibility in his timing because of traffic and emergencies at work?" The emotional interests can be articulated and the negotiations can proceed.

Although searching for underlying interests and then framing the problem in terms of interests may be helpful to the PC and the parents, the parents often will need help in moving from their positions to interest-based negotiations. The PC's thoughtful and consistent restatement of impartiality as to the parents and commitment as to the children's needs is crucial. The motivation for each parent to consider the other parent's needs in solving the problem is the positive impact that a successful and peaceful settlement will have on the children. The PC must remind parents of the reason for resolving the issue, that is, their children are experiencing distress because of the conflict at transfers and the conflict must be eliminated for the health and welfare of their children.

Build Empathy

Empathy has been previously described in Chapter 2 as the act of identifying with the feelings or thoughts of another person. Parents stuck in high conflict, especially highly narcissistically vulnerable parents, often are unable to empathize with the other parent or even with their children. The first step in building empathy between the parents is for the PC to truly empathize with each parent. By putting him/herself in the shoes of a parent, the PC can help determine the best way to go about helping the parents to put themselves in the shoes of the other parent. By reversing roles and contemplating what the other parent is feeling and experiencing, parents are sometimes able to feel empathy for one another. The PC should also attempt to build empathy for the children and always talk about what the children must be experiencing because of their parents' conflict.

The PC can also play the role of the "devil's advocate," that is, present a case against a parent's position and hold it up to its worst light. However, in doing so a PC risks a parent's ire and the perception that the PC is taking sides. A devil's advocate role is best used in separate meetings with one parent and only when that parent trusts the PC and accepts the PC playing that role. It is often very difficult to help one parent understand the other parent because of irrational thinking and narcissistic tendencies, as discussed earlier. Empathy requires a parent to have a strong sense of self and his/her own boundaries. However, the PC can and must be an advocate for the children and their needs. The PC must insist that the parents always attempt to see the parental conflict through the eyes of their children, even if the parents seem to be unable to have empathy for each other.

Change the Parents' Perspectives of the Situation

In high-conflict situations, feelings are usually more important than thoughts. Each parent has a different perspective of the relevant marital and family history, current facts, their own grievances, and the goals and intentions of the other parent (Fisher et al. 1994, p. 25). Changing perspectives of the situation begins with helping each parent understand and empathize with the other parent. Because of the intense fear, which underlies many parenting disputes, of losing the children to the other parent, changing the way parents view one another is extremely difficult. When the PC observes that parents are misperceiving each other, the PC should attempt to correct these perceptions to permit negotiations between them to move forward (Moore 1996, p. 169). It is easier to work on parental misperceptions in separate meetings rather than in joint meetings with the parents because of the risk that the PC will seem biased for or against one of the parents. The PC can help each parent identify perceptions about the other parent and assess the accuracy or inaccuracy of these perceptions.

In our example, when the mother perceives that the father's tardiness at transfers is done solely to show that he has no respect for her time and individual activities, the PC can help articulate this to the mother and discuss with her the factual basis that the father has presented for his lack of punctuality, that is, his job time unpredictability and unforeseen traffic jams. The PC can also talk to the father about his behavior and the resentment that it triggers in the mother, as well as her perceptions. The goal is to help the parents shift their perceptions from always seeing the other parent as attacking to seeing that the other parent may have behaviors that, although negative, are not directed specifically against the offended parent. This is tricky because the perceptions are held not only because of past history, but also because they validate the parent holding them. It is difficult to give up a judgment against the "enemy" if it might then throw blame back on the parent with the misperception.

Help Parents Change Their Behaviors

It may be difficult, if not impossible, to change the perceptions that one parent has about the other, but the PC can help each parent change certain behaviors that trigger the worst behaviors in the other parent. Angry people fail to hear what others have to say, especially if it does not validate their own perceptions of the situation. However, the PC can acknowledge to the complaining parent, in a separate meeting, that the problems he/she perceives indeed exist. By then emphasizing that the behavior in the other person may not be able to be changed, the discussion can shift to how this parent can change his or her own behavior to benefit the children. A behavior change may involve responding differently to the behaviors of the other parent that always push buttons. The PC can also explore with each parent his or her own behavior that triggers negative behavior in the other parent. Discussions about the power of positive reinforcement with the other parent can be somewhat effective at this time. The PC should reinforce positive behavior changes in the parents often and consistently as such changes, even minute ones, occur.

In our example, the mother consistently complains that the father is late for transfers of the children by reminding him that his whole family of origin has no sense of punctuality and are insensitive clods. The father then responds that the mother is overly compulsive regarding time, and relates that back to her own uptight and rigid mother. He then continues to be late in picking up the children because it demonstrates his independence from his controlling ex-wife. In discussing the dynamic with the mother, the PC can help her to curb the negative statements to the father about his family as well as to develop strategies for dealing with the father's lack of punctuality. The PC can explore with the father his motivations in being late, the effect of that behavior on the mother, and how that particular behavior can be avoided for the good of the children.

Set Limits

When parents act out and the PC is unable to rationally change harmful behavior, the PC must set limits for the well-being of the children. For example, if the transfers of the children for parenting time are always conflictual and negative, the PC can structure transitions to eliminate contact between the parents by having the transfers take place at a neutral site, such as the day-care center, where one parent does not have to wait for the other parent to appear and pick up the children. The PC will also have to set and enforce limits regarding the use of the parenting coordination process. Some parents will call every day, if allowed, just to vent about the other parent. This is usually not helpful and will only alienate the PC against that parent. Parents in high-conflict situations need structure and, although they will chafe within the limits imposed upon them, they cannot be flexible without taking liberties, which are then seen as aggressive acts by the other parent. Limit setting, process, and structure are tools used to focus parents on the business of parenting.

THE TOOLS OF THE TRADE

It is essential that a Parenting Coordinator's role be based upon expertise and training. Some Parenting Coordinators are comfortable intervening at many levels; others are uncomfortable with specific techniques and prefer to keep their roles circumscribed. The primary types of interventions are reviewed below. Consider your own comfort level, background, and training as you read through these descriptions and seek additional training or supervision before attempting an uncomfortable role, or if you prefer, coordinate with a professional with the needed skills to act.

Mediation

Mediation is a process of dispute resolution that uses a neutral third party to facilitate the negotiations of the parties. A mediator uses the techniques of conflict management, as discussed previously, with the goal of allowing the parties self-determination of their dispute. A PC usually serves as a mediator but a PC is also an educator, an interface to other systems and professionals, and a decision maker, or arbitrator, if that role is a comfortable one. Thus the PC is a proactive, goal-focused mediator.

Arbitration

Arbitration is a process of dispute resolution that uses a neutral third party to make decisions for parties who cannot agree. Arbitration authority can be given to the PC to use in situations in which the PC has tried mediation skills to help the parents reach settlement themselves, but they have reached an impasse and voluntary settlement is not possible. In some situations, the arbitration authority may be allocated to another professional, such as a Med-Arbiter, Guardian *ad litem*, or a Special Master, depending on the practice in the parents' jurisdiction. A professional should not undertake to become a PC with arbitration authority if making decisions for other people is not a comfortable role. The PC must be firm, confident, well grounded in theory and practice, and have a history of successful involvement in high-conflict cases in order to survive the parents' wrath when the arbitrator makes a decision that the parents dislike. However, the ability to make decisions so that the dispute can be resolved and the family can move forward provides the parents with a much-needed finality that mediation alone does not provide. A combination of mediation and arbitration is often very helpful. Depending upon the law of a particular state, arbitrated decisions need to be put in writing, filed with the court, and made a part of the court record.

Referral

The PC should have the authority and knowledge to refer parents to other professionals or agencies such as therapists, evaluators, attorneys, or parent educators. This requires that the PC develop a referral network within his community of services for parents and children. If the PC is aware of outside support resources for specific difficulties, a referral is often appreciated by both parents. For example, an educational specialist might be consulted for assessment of kindergarten readiness or learning disabilities.

Communication between the Parents

One of the interventions most frequently performed by the PC is that of being a communication link between the parents. When parents are unable to communicate directly in person, or on the telephone, and when even written notes or e-mail messages are problematic, the PC may be called upon to relay messages between the parents. Sometimes this process of communication becomes the modus operandi on a regular basis, or it may be used only in crisis or when enough time does not exist for the nondirect communication that some parents are normally allowed. The techniques of reframing, building empathy, and other conflict-management techniques can strategically be used when relaying messages and can ease the animosity tremendously. The goal is not to simply transfer messages word for word, but to reframe them in terms of interests rather than positions so that mediation of the issues is possible.

Communication between the Parents and Children

Children often need help in communicating with one or both of their parents. The PC can translate the children's concerns into interests that the parents can hear and meet. The PC is not a therapist to the children but a trusted adult who advocates for them. Regular meetings with the children are helpful in refocusing from the parents' complaints to the needs of the children.

A PC also can keep lines of communication open between one parent and the children when there is an extraordinary degree of animosity and anger. The PC can be the recipient of the children's mail or gifts at holiday time to assure that they are delivered to the children when there are accusations that the residential parent is intercepting or destroying mail or not delivering gifts. The PC can also place phone calls to an out-of-state parent if calls are being denied or not honored. The PC will find, as time goes by, what the triggers are for each parent and re-interpreting and re-framing communication becomes easier and the receiving parent more grateful for civilly delivered information.

REPORTING

A PC may be ordered by the court to provide reports to the court or to attorneys. This raises practice issues regarding confidentiality and testifying in court. The PC should be certain to take good notes, not only to be able to report accurately but also to help in strategizing the case. Reports should focus on the children's needs and discuss recommendations for a parenting plan that will reduce the conflict between the parents and improve the parenting of the children. Specificity is important, but assigning blame should be avoided, if possible. The court needs, however, to know if a protective order is necessary for the safety of the children. Suggestions about pathways to repair and recovery are more helpful and welcomed than proposals about punitive measures.

COACHING

The PC can be especially useful in coaching parents on how to negotiate and communicate with the other parent. Parents often react to each other in the same unproductive and dysfunctional manner as when they were married. In separate sessions or on the telephone, the PC can suggest timing, communication techniques, and specific wording for a parent to use and also advise on how to avoid pushing the buttons of the other parent. Upon a parent's request, the PC can also review correspondence prior to sending for the tone of the letter. For example, an angry, hostile letter from a dad demanding a parenting time schedule change will not get him the results he wants, particularly when an issue for the mom is that the dad always has tried to control and dominate her. When the mom perceives "demands" rather than "requests" for a change, she will absolutely refuse to be flexible because the letter triggers all of her issues of independence, domination, and subservience. Dad will need to make requests, not demands, and acknowledge that Mom has the power to accept or reject the requested schedule change. Often parents are totally unaware of the emotional quality of the words chosen for their communication. A letter with a businesslike yet collaborative and cordial tone is more apt to elicit a positive response. Using basic, commonsense communication skills coupled with a thorough analysis of the triggers of each parent, the PC can assist the parents in avoiding unnecessary conflict. Years of distrust and knee-jerk reactions cannot be eliminated quickly, or in some cases at all, but coaching has the benefit of being an intervention that is individually supportive and acknowledging of the strengths of the coached parent.

Part III

The High-Conflict Model In Use

8

Practical Applications

Working with high-conflict families requires more than most professionals realize. One should carefully consider suitability to the role and willingness to undertake the demands of such a practice before embarking into this new territory. Considerations should be made of the character traits and professional skills required. One should be honest in his/her self-appraisal. The work will be demanding, time consuming, and frustrating. Progress will be slow and at moments it may seem that there is regression rather than progression. Crises will be an ever-present part of the Parenting Coordinator's (PC's) professional life. Parents will deluge a PC with their emotions; these may be rageful, mournful, threatening, whiny, or passive/aggressive. A PC will find it necessary to draw upon the utmost character strength and cleverness. Certain personality and professional traits are critical in getting through the difficult moments. The PC must assess his/her own patience, sense of humor, capacity to set limits, tolerance to absorb rageful outbursts and blaming, and compassion for children to be able to expose him-/herself to the conflict so that they might be shielded from it. There should also be a wonderful colleague with whom to share concerns.

WHICH SERVICES TO PROVIDE

The first step is determining what kind of services will be offered. In defining the scope of the PC's work, it is crucial to consider the PC's professional training and experience as well as individual strengths and weaknesses. One of the most common mistakes is attempting to take on too many roles within the same family. This seems especially to be a danger for mental health professionals who have clinical experience and expertise with children and also have training in mediation or conflict resolution. Defining the PC's role is one of the most important caveats.

As you have seen in this manual, there are many different roles a PC can assume with any given family:

- assessor
- mediator
- arbitrator
- med-arbiter
- case coordinator
- communication facilitator
- parent education
- parents' coach
- guidance counselor to children around divorce-related areas

It is extremely important that the PC decide which of these possible roles is suitable. Each role requires different skills, and some require specific training. A PC should take on only the roles for which he/she is qualified.

A special caveat regards the children: If the PC meets with the children, the children may bring underlying issues into the process. The PC must be careful to respond with empathy but to refer the child to an individual therapist for issues more serious than those that could be characterized as adjustment issues to the divorce and high conflict. Trauma, anxiety, depression, and conduct disorders commonly result from high-conflict divorce. These are more serious than adjustment issues and require an individual therapist. The PC should not be tempted to take on the role of psychotherapist, as it will only confuse and complicate the relationship-building role the PC serves between the child and parents.

TEAM OR SOLO WORK

Parenting coordination can be conducted by a team or done solo. Many professionals prefer the team approach but it is more expensive for the family, and this is not a service covered by insurance. There are advantages to each model and the PC will want to weigh these carefully. If a PC works alone, it eliminates the often time-consuming and cumbersome task of coordinating the work with another professional. The PC avoids the tendency of high-conflict parents to "split" the two professionals into the "good guy" and "bad guy." On the other hand, if the PC works with another professional as part of a parenting-coordination team, the intensity of the work can be shared and the responsibility for decision making shared. It is possible to structure a model that is a combination of team and solo work. For example, the initial assessment could be done as a team and the ongoing parenting-coordination work done by one of the professionals with the other moving into the arbitration role, as necessary.

CONTRACTS AND AGREEMENTS

It is essential that the PC construct a contract with both parents prior to beginning work. The Parenting-Coordinator Agreement is the main contract with the parents. The PC may decide to have a standard agreement for use with all families, but it is wiser to customize the agreement to each individual situation. This agreement spells out the specific services the PC will provide and the conditions of these services. The topics to consider having in an agreement include:

- the terms of any stipulations or court orders regarding parenting coordination
- the specific issues that will be dealt with in parenting coordination (i.e., the parenting time schedule, decisions about extracurricular activities, education)
- the process by which the work will be accomplished (i.e., individual versus joint meetings with the parents, involvement of the children, telephone versus in-person contact, inclusion of new spouses or significant others, and crisis management)
- the role or roles of the PC (i.e., assessor, mediator, arbitrator, communication facilitator, educator, case coordinator)
- type of decision-making authority the PC will have, if any
- the specific issues that may be decided (arbitrated) by the PC and the issues that will be referred to an outside arbitrator or to the courts. These issues may or may not be the same as the issues the PC is asked to help parents decide for themselves.
- to whom information may be released
- from whom information may be gathered
- the length of time the PC will serve in this role
- the conditions under which the PC may resign or be dismissed

- the means for finding a replacement PC
- confidentiality (see additional comments below)
- fees (see additional comments below)

In formulating the agreement, the PC should remain as neutral and equidistant from the attorneys representing the parties as possible. It is as important not to ally with one attorney as it is not to ally with one parent. The contract is with the parents, not the attorneys.

The PC should not become emotionally invested in the contracting process. One parent may be very frustrating to deal with and the PC may feel that this parent is preventing getting on with the task at hand. The other parent may be calling frequently, inquiring whether the reluctant parent has signed the agreement or sent the retainer. The PC should beware of the temptation to side with the apparently more reasonable parent. It is important to treat both parents with courtesy and calm professional distance. The PC may need to let one parent know that the PC cannot pressure the other parent to proceed against his/her will. If necessary, refer that parent back to his or her attorney and let the attorney apply the pressure. The PC can call the reluctant party to convey the other parent's wish to proceed, but anything more puts the PC in the position of advocating for one side over the other.

It is not uncommon for the parenting coordinator to be presented with an immediate problem to solve before the agreement is structured and signed. It is critical to get all of the intake and contracting issues taken care of first before intervening in any way. Although the contracting process may take a long time, it is well worth the wait to get a solid agreement on which to base involvement with the family. The PC should avoid the temptation to help the parents settle any issue, large or small, prior to having a signed agreement. If the PC succumbs to the pressure to help prematurely, without clear agreements in place with both parents, he/she risks unwittingly setting precedents or forming alliances that may later be regretted. Sometimes this can even preclude future effective work with the family. The PC must take the time needed to work through a thoughtful and individually tailored agreement for the family situation.

Chapters 11 and 12 contain a number of sample agreements that can be customized for particular situations. In some states, the PC can elect not to arbitrate directly but to refer that decision-making power to a Special Master (see Chapter 13).

FEE AGREEMENTS

The fee agreement spells out the exact charges for the parenting-coordination services and who is responsible to pay them, including who pays for different kinds of sessions, such as sessions with only one parent, those with both parents, and those with the children. Each parent either pays for any sessions he/she has alone with the PC and the parents split the cost of any joint sessions and sessions with the children, or all fees may be split. Occasionally, there is a court order that specifies what percentage of the charges each parent is to pay; this must be respected. The PC should try to structure an arrangement in which each parent pays at least a minimal amount so that both parties have an investment in the process.

It is important to determine what unit of time will be used for various charges. This will be important as time will be spent returning calls, preparing written documents, collaborating with other professionals, and reviewing written material.

Some parenting coordinators obtain a retainer to be charged against and replenished when it reaches a certain minimum. If you use the retainer approach, be clear in specifying how much is needed initially from each parent, how charges will be billed against the retainer, and when the account must be replenished. Any excess moneys should be refunded at the end of the process. If the PC anticipates that one or both parties are likely to be dissatisfied with the services or decisions made, the retainer method should seriously be considered. Disappointed and angry parents tend to withhold payment, leaving the PC in the uncomfortable situation of deciding whether to terminate services when the children may be benefiting.

ASSESSING FEES DIFFERENTIALLY

Some PCs like to have the capacity to assess fees differentially—rather than in the usual proportion—when one client acts out severely or causes the PC to spend an inordinate amount of time on an issue. There are certainly times when parents in high conflict try to use the PC process as yet another weapon with which to hurt the other parent. Some PCs put a clause in their fee agreement that states that the PC reserves the right to change the proportion of fees charged to each parent for certain kinds of infractions. Then, for instance, if one parent spends a great deal of time on a minor issue and requires the PC to read volumes of documents, thus incurring more charges to the other parent as well, the PC could decide to assess the acting-out parent all of the fees associated with this activity or a larger-than-usual percentage. Other PCs do not do this, believing that deciding which issues are frivolous or minor, who is wasting the PC's time, or who is acting out more is a slippery slope for the PC to walk and keep one's balance. Changing the usual fee arrangements for such instances certainly can in and of itself engender more battles between high-conflict parents—and with the PC. If you decide to reserve the right to assess fees differentially at times, be sure to inform parents up front and have a clear clause in your agreement. Be aware that the parent charged more may well feel treated unfairly. Decisions regarding acting out and the importance of any given issue certainly involve at least a small measure, if not a large amount, of subjective judgment. One other option is have a clause in your agreement that allows the PC to tell the parties if an inordinate amount of time is being taken on any given issue (see Chapter 11). Then if the PC alerts the parents to such an occurrence, the PC can add that if it continues, the parent responsible for the continuance will be billed all or more of the associated charges. This gives the offending parent an opportunity to stop before incurring additional charges. It also may help preserve the fairness of the PC's stance.

CONFIDENTIALITY

One of the most important decisions the PC needs to make in constructing an agreement is that of defining the parameters of confidentiality. It is critical to have agreements with all the parties addressing to whom the PC may release information and from whom the PC may gather information. Some of the specific decisions that must be made are:

- Which other professionals, such as psychotherapists, teachers, or health-care providers, will be authorized to share information about the family with the PC?
- What information so gathered can be shared with the parents?
- What information shared by one parent may be shared with the other parent? It is often important with high-conflict families to share only what is healing, not what is hurtful.
- What are the ethical and legal considerations regarding confidentiality of practicing as a PC in the state?

Another crucial aspect of confidentiality issues is what information gained in the process of parenting coordination can or must be shared with the court in any subsequent legal proceedings. If the PC has arbitration power, arbitration awards should be written and sent not only to both parents and their attorneys but also to the court for confirmation into a court order. Many arbitrators attempt to keep their own notes (which include information regarding the parties' behavior during the PC process, for instance) confidential and to use some discretion about the details that are included in the written award. If one is functioning as a Special Advocate in Colorado, the court expects a report with the results of the Special Advocate's investigation and recommendations. Obviously in these situations, the PC must be clear with the family that information cannot be kept confidential. Only if the PC does not have any decision-making authority and is only mediating may it be feasible to keep the parenting-coordination process confidential.

Of course, any mental health professionals working as PCs must report any concerns about imminent danger to self or others or suspicions of child abuse to the appropriate social service agency or the police (see "Allegations of Abuse" later in this chapter for more information).

STIPULATED AGREEMENTS

Some jurisdictions actually court order parenting-coordination service (see Chapter 14). If a PC is aware that a case will be court ordered to his/her practice, the PC may want to provide input regarding the content of the court order. It helps if the attorneys involved with the family understand the parenting-coordination process in general and the PC's specific procedures and policies. The order is, therefore, most likely to be worded in a manner that is compatible with the PC's working style and practices. If a case has been court ordered to a specific parenting coordinator, then that PC is subject to the order and must comply. The attorneys and especially the Guardian *ad litem*, if one has been appointed, may be very helpful in this area.

Most parents decide voluntarily to use parenting-coordination services and then, with the help of their attorneys, stipulate to this. This is strongly recommended as a means of securing the cooperation of difficult parents. This stipulation can contain crucial details of the PC roles and functions and the responsibilities of each parent. Although this may duplicate much of the content of the PC's agreement with the family, it will add substantial weight to the agreement because it will have the status of being a court order once it is filed with the court.

In Colorado, the court, by a motion of either party, may appoint a special advocate who can investigate, report, and make recommendations (see Chapter 15). The Special Advocate can thus recommend a PC for the benefit of the children and/or to contain the conflict between the parents.

ISSUES EXCLUDED
FROM PARENT COORDINATION

The PC will want to decide if there are any issues with which he/she will not deal as a PC. One issue is change of custody. In most states, only the court can officially change the custody determination. Consequently, the PC will want the agreement to specify that legal custody will not be a part of the process. Out-of-state moves or relocation issues are serious and difficult to structure. If the PC does not have knowledge and experience in this area, this may be excluded from the agreement. The PC should be clear with families about these issues, or others that determine the conditions of the PC's role. State law may limit the issues in which a PC may be involved. The PC should be well informed of what he/she may or may not do, and seek consultation from an attorney if necessary.

INTAKE PROCESS

How the PC handles the initial stages of a case can make an enormous impact on the work of parenting coordination. It is advisable to be clear about how the following issues will be handled:

- Who can make appointments? Sometimes attorneys will call and want to set up appointments for their clients. Some PCs may wish to accommodate this practice; others may wish to have the parties make their own appointments.
- Will parents be offered an initial appointment in which services are described and any questions or concerns are discussed? Will such an appointment be at no charge?
- Will such an offer be made to each parent individually or only to both parents together (to ensure that one has said exactly the same thing to both parties)? Will the initial appointment include the parents' attorneys or a Guardian *ad litem*?
- What materials will prospective clients or referral sources get (e.g., a brochure on services or copies of agreements that might be used)?
- How much information will be given on the telephone? Parents who have been in high conflict often have long stories to tell and may want the PC's reaction to a number of things. Initial telephone calls may be limited to basic information and an offer to schedule an informational meeting. On the other hand, parents may need to know that the PC has heard them before they are willing to consider hiring the PC. This may be true especially if arbitration powers for the parenting coordinator are being considered.
- At what point will the PC give an opinion or offer advice? Frequently there is a pressing issue that has precipitated the referral for parenting coordination and parents often want to get this issue resolved right away. The PC needs to be prepared to tell parents what must be done (for instance, signing agreements and paying retainers) before they can expect issues to be addressed. What agreements

must the parents sign before services commence? Will a
retainer be required?

It is not uncommon for six months to a year to pass between
the initial telephone call and the signing of agreements. This can
happen even when cases are court ordered into parenting
coordination. Often one party is eager to start services and the
other is reluctant or causes delays. Then when the reluctant party
decides to move forward, the eager party may suddenly become
the hesitant one. It is helpful for the PC to remember that
high-conflict couples do not do well making decisions together,
and deciding to engage the services of a PC requires them to do
just that. The PC needs to keep a calm, professional demeanor
and be careful not to respond to provocation or insistence that
something be done "immediately." The PC should keep the focus
on the parents' need to decide whether they want the services of
a PC. If the case is court ordered, a letter to the attorneys
notifying them of the status of the case may help.

HOW WILL THE CHILDREN BE INVOLVED?

The amount of involvement for the children in the parenting-
coordination process is based on many factors. First, the PC must
assess his/her own expertise, skills, and training in child development and the effect of divorce on children. The PC may elect
to "know" the children solely through information provided by
the parents, teachers, therapists, Guardians *ad litem*, and others. If
the PC is comfortable interviewing and working with children, it
is typically best to meet the individuals whom your work is meant
to benefit. Often the children wish to have a voice and there is no
avenue for their input unless they have a therapist. Reluctant to
share their honest opinions with either parent, the children may
be hopelessly caught in the intensity of the conflict with no

guidance, empathy, or coping skills. Most children are grateful to learn that someone is working to contain the conflict between their parents and is supportive of their right to grow up healthy. Contact with the children can take different forms:

- Meeting the children initially and at selected intervals to form an impression of their coping capacity, individual issues, and reactions to the divorce and conflict.
- Assessing the children to comprehensively determine their developmental level, coping, resiliency, and need for individual or group therapy.
- Scheduling periodic meetings to keep up-to-date with the children's adjustment.
- Actively involving the children in the parenting-coordination process. This might be considered if the children's relationship with one or both parents is highly conflicted, if the children are taking sides, or if there are serious endangerment or impaired-parenting issues. The older the children, the more likely they are to desire and benefit from inclusion in the process.
- Educating the children about ways to manage the conflict, free themselves from the conflict, and be able to involve themselves in age-appropriate activities with peers.
- Supporting the children in the pain of the divorce process and in having their wishes and needs respected in the time-share planning and special circumstances unique to creating a tailor-made plan for their family post-divorce.
- Giving the children permission to call at any time to discuss a divorce concern, to problem solve, or to raise an issue for further discussion. The sense that someone is available to them is very reassuring to the children caught in the middle, and they tend to use the permission to call wisely, for just cause, and not to abuse the privilege as their parents are likely to do.

RELATIONSHIP TO
MENTAL HEALTH PROFESSIONALS

The frequency and nature of the contact between the PC and any psychotherapists treating family members is best decided on a case-by-case basis. Of course, appropriate releases of information or a specific court order authorizing exchange of information is required. Any psychotherapist treating one of the adults may provide an in-depth understanding of the intrapsychic dynamics that trigger the client. The therapist can often illuminate the "red buttons" by giving the PC information about the life experiences that contributed to their creation. The PC may broaden the therapist's understanding of the client and distortions in the client's communications about the other parent. When an arbitrated decision is made, the PC may wish to inform the therapist of the facts as well as the reasoning behind the decision. The client can be helped to accept the decision through his or her own therapeutic process if the therapist so wishes.

When one or more of the children have a therapist, this can be a great boon to the PC. The child's therapist often is greatly relieved that the parents have someone other than the therapist to whom to turn for advice and decision making. The PC's involvement in parenting issues can leave the therapist free to do therapy and to keep a better alliance with both parents and the child. Often a therapist can give the PC vital information about the child, such as the child's feelings, perceptions, coping abilities, and needs, which greatly aids the PC in decision making. The PC may choose to know the child predominately through contact with the therapist in fact.

Therapists (especially parents' therapists), however, can occasionally become strongly allied with a client. One of the effective aspects of psychotherapy is the therapist's ability to empathize with the client and understand life and events from that individual's point of view. This can cause the therapist to gradually share the client's perceptions of the other parent.

Strongly allied therapists, in this sense, can complicate the PC process if they become part of the tribal warfare. Often, they are unaware of their contribution to the ongoing conflict.

The PC must use professional judgment in determining the extent and frequency of the contact with the therapists for either parent.

RELATIONSHIP TO LEGAL PROFESSIONALS

The PC should be clear in regard to relating to the various legal professionals who may be involved with the family. A Guardian *ad litem* already may have been appointed and one or both parents may have attorneys.

The responsibility of the Guardian *ad litem* may overlap to some extent with the responsibilities of a PC. Roles can be divided or coordinated, but it is critical to form a working alliance for the benefit of the children and the sake of the family as a whole. The PC and GAL must determine what information will be shared and coordinate their roles.

It is crucial that there be an open and frank discussion between the attorney and parenting coordinator about what roles each will play in the family. The attorney must be fully informed of the role of the PC in order to properly advise a client and fulfill ethical and legal duties to the client. The following practical tips may be helpful in guiding the PC's relationship with the respective attorneys:

- The PC must contact the attorneys before beginning work and be clear about the role of the PC and the nature of the PC agreement.
- The PC must educate the attorney about the services of a PC. Many attorneys are unfamiliar with what a PC does.
- The PC must share the PC agreement with the attorneys. Any changes to the agreement should be negotiated

between the PC, the parties, and their attorneys. When the PC has arbitration authority, the arbitrator process should be clearly delineated, including the impact of relevant state law on such issues as whether the arbitration is binding and what avenues for appeal exist.

- Attorneys who are supportive of the parenting-coordination process can encourage clients to continue their participation even when upset by a ruling of the PC. It may be helpful, if working with supportive attorneys, for the PC to provide each with a progress report without revealing any of the "he said, she said" that goes on in the office. All attorneys need to be included in written communication. Written documents can be sent to the attorneys directly or the parents can be informed that it is their responsibility to share any written material with their respective attorneys. Any decisions reached in mediation or arbitration, however, must be written as formal documents and provided to both parents, all attorneys involved, and, if appropriate, filed with the court (see Chapter 16).

- It is important to set limits for attorneys, particularly those who are overidentified with their clients. A clear-cut understanding of the professional-to-professional role needs to be agreed upon and respected. Often this occurs only after someone has worked with an attorney over several cases. A mutual trust is established and talk can be freer. If this is not the case, the PC must be careful to be firm in setting limits. For instance, if the attorney calls after each session with a running commentary about the client's needs or the general level of the PC's functioning, it is time for the PC to be firm, set a limit, and tell the attorney that the PC is the one guiding the process. This is easier with attorneys who are known and trusted.

- Attorneys can help enormously when a PC makes a decision or arbitrated award that offends the client. The attorney can be a sympathetic listener, join in with the "ain't it awful," but then gently encourage a return to the PC process, reminding the client that it is cheaper and less public than court, and that one does not always win in court.

Simply put, team playing with the attorneys is essential for parenting-coordination success.

PHONE CALLS

High-conflict families tend to initiate an inordinate number of phone calls. Often a minor issue takes on the flavor of an emergency. Issues with which most divorced couples can cope become crises that the high-conflict couple believes warrant the intervention of the PC. Some individuals truly abuse the voice-messaging system and use it to leave long, contentious calls complaining about the other parent. Deciding in advance how telephone calls will be handled and billed is essential. The following issues, at a minimum, need to be thought through and communicated by the PC, preferably in the written agreement, to the parents:

- The PC must decide how available he/she is willing to be to these often needy families. It is very important that a PC recognizes his/her own capacity to tolerate numerous telephone calls. These calls may be placed during transition times, which are typically after hours, on weekends, and during holidays. Often each call is identified as an emergency although most mental health professionals would not define them as such. The typical "emergency call" from a high-conflict family involves a complaint about the manner in which the other parent did something, failed to do something, or disappointed the children. Ground rules about what constitutes an emergency that will be responded to quickly must be defined. Strategies for handling the inconveniences of divorced life can be handled in the next meeting and are rarely a true emergency.

- The PC must decide which issues can be handled on the telephone and which must be dealt with in person. It is often useful for the PC to tell the parents that he/she reserves the right to use his/her professional discretion to decide these matters.
- The PC must be very clear about how time spent on the telephone will be charged.

RECORD KEEPING

The PC must consider carefully what kinds of records to keep. Enough information should always be kept on file to document accurately and carefully what has been worked on with the parents. The PC may log all contacts, including the time of telephone calls and the specifics of messages. High-conflict clients are often quite litigious and it is important and reasonable to protect oneself.

If the PC decides to write an assessment of the family, thoughts about the children, or dynamic formulation, he/she must remember that once written material is given to a party, the PC no longer has control over its distribution. The only sure way to keep a report from being used in a destructive manner is not to commit it to paper. This must be balanced with the need for clear and concise information being produced in a form usable to a party and/or the other professionals involved.

As discussed previously, any decisions reached in mediation or arbitration must be in writing as formal documents and given to both parents, all attorneys including the GAL, and, if appropriate, filed with the court.

ALLEGATIONS OF ABUSE

One of the most emotionally charged and difficult issues that can be raised during the parenting-coordination process is an allegation of abuse by one of the parents. The PC must know what his/her legal and ethical responsibilities are in these situations. The allegations could be false or true but regardless, the PC must be well informed about the requirements of the jurisdiction for reporting such allegations to either the Department of Social Services or the police department for further investigation. This is not an easy determination to make because of the complexities involved with high-conflict families. One parent, desperate to limit the children's time with the other parent, may make false reports of physical or sexual abuse or neglect. A parent may also have a legitimate concern that the other parent is abusive in some way. Often the situation is quite gray—one parent may be somewhat inadequate, the other quite fearful, and the evidence is equivocal about whether the children have been abused. The PC must walk a fine line—consider seriously the possibility that the children are in fact in need of protection while simultaneously guard against overreacting and taking action that will unnecessarily derail the parenting-coordination process.

The PC may wish to consult a colleague before deciding how to handle allegations. It is often very helpful to call the local Department of Social Services and ask the intake worker for a consultation. The PC can describe the situation without using the clients' names and ask the intake worker whether this situation should be reported and how it would be handled by the department. Frequently, allegations of abuse in divorce situations are given low priority for investigation. The PC should carefully document what he/she is told by the intake worker, especially if the PC is advised not to make a formal report. If the PC is subsequently challenged for this decision, it is important to be able to demonstrate that appropriate steps were taken in the situation. If a formal report needs to be made, the PC has the opportunity to request of the intake worker whatever involvement the PC believes is advisable in the investigation process.

SUPERVISED VISITATION

Supervised visitation is sometimes necessary to assure the safety of children both physically and psychologically. Occasionally, a supervised setting is used when allegations of abuse have been made but have not been formally investigated. This can assure that the parent–child relationship is continued in a safe manner during the investigative period, which can grow into months in some instances.

Although the PC cannot make the ultimate decision regarding the use of supervised visitation, he or she may be asked to make a recommendation. Weighing the risk of harm to a child during visitation versus the emotional harm of suspending parent–child contact represents a serious determination, especially when all of the facts have not been gathered and a full investigation has not been completed. Recognizing this, the Honorable Sean M. Dunphy, Chief Justice of the Massachusetts Probate and Family Court, appointed a task force of legal and mental health professionals chaired by Hon. Arline S. Rotman to create guidelines for the appropriate use of supervised visitation. These outstanding guidelines, "Supervised Visitation Risk Assessment for Judges" can be found in Chapter 17. Not only do these guidelines present different levels of supervised visitation, they also specify child and parental factors to consider in making this arduous decision.

Supervised visitation is typically a temporary solution to a grave situation. Often it is ordered for a period of time and then abruptly terminated with the assumption that the endangering circumstances have been addressed. Unfortunately, the serious problems that lead up to supervised visitation are not easily remedied. It is critical that the children have the opportunity to gradually move into a more normalized visitation program with a professional monitoring the children's sense of emotional well-being and physical safety. The PC who already has a relationship with the children and family is an ideal professional for guiding the movement from supervised to unsupervised visitation. Guidelines, as well as a time frame, were developed by Nancy Gary, Psy.D., a psychologist who frequently served in this capacity and found judges, attorneys, and parents expressing a need for a paradigm for moving away from supervision (see Chapter 17, Form 17–3).

Some children in supervised visitation have suffered such severe and repeated traumatization that a return to normalized visitation may not be possible. Johnston and Straus (1999) state that "it is essential to pay attention to and protect against the profound consequences of psychologically unsafe relationships" (pp. 144–145). The children who use supervised visitation services are highly vulnerable and frightened and often depleted in coping resources. The adults in their lives have not kept them safe, and to expect these children to trust an unfamiliar supervisor to provide safety may be unrealistic. Recognizing the child who is experiencing greater distress rather than healing and recovery is essential to prevent retraumatization. Johnston and Straus (1999) offer the following guidelines as a "nonexhaustive and nonprescriptive list" (p. 155) of symptoms that might signal a need to suspend contact:

- The child repeatedly refuses to come to the visitation site, or once there refuses to see the noncustodial parent.
- The child is chronically distressed during the visit, showing signs of fear.
- The custodial parent reports a serious and pervasive decline in the child's functioning in other settings such as school and home, which is verified by other objective observers.

- Developmental milestones that had been achieved are lost by younger children after the supervised visitation was initiated.

ESTABLISHING WORKING RELATIONSHIPS
WITH DIFFICULT CLIENTS

Working with high-conflict families means working with difficult clients. It is common to find that many professionals have already been involved with these families, and some may have terminated the relationship because of the difficulties entailed in making and maintaining good working alliances. Regardless of the feelings the client evokes, the PC must do his/her best to remember the following:

- Every client is due respect and empathy.
- Underneath most "bad" behavior is pain—shame, hurt, anger, or rage, which the client is trying unsuccessfully to manage.
- Emotional regulation can vary widely within one person. For example, one can have the capacity to be successful at a demanding profession while having a total inability to control aggressive impulses around an ex-spouse.
- Most of the time, the client is doing the best he or she can.

To establish effective relationships with difficult clients, the PC must invoke the following techniques:

- Treat these clients with the same respect and courtesy as with his/her favorite clients.
- Try to understand the world through the client's eyes.
- Find out what the client wants to accomplish.
- Actively ally with any of the client's goals that you feel are appropriate. This is one of the PC's most powerful tools.

- Try to empathize with how the client feels.
- Identify any areas of good functioning, especially in parenting. This will form a strong basis for an alliance.
- Do not underestimate areas of low functioning (even failure of reality testing or psychosis) just because the client has many areas of high functioning, such as in a career.
- Recognize that the client cannot always control his or her behavior.
- The PC is unlikely to change the client in any fundamental way no matter how much he/she would like to. Humility in this area is crucial.
- Set realistic behavioral goals.
- The PC should know his/her own limits and boundaries and operate within them.
- Expect battles, frustrations, setbacks, and explosions.
- Do not withdraw emotionally at difficult times. Engaging with the client at these times is one of the most important keys to success.
- Tell the client the truth about perceptions of the problem, but speak it with compassion.
- Be prepared to meet affect with affect. This may require more expressiveness and disclosure than normal.
- Make sure the client knows when an exaggeration of a concern or a manipulation has been detected, but do not berate the client.
- The PC should think of him/herself as a good parent— one who is caring; sets appropriate limits and expectations; motivates; models empathy, honesty, and integrity; handles conflicts fairly; and confronts with compassion the pain that underlies the "bad" behavior.

Parenting coordination is intense and time consuming. The PC should not take on more of these cases than can be handled at any one time. These are exhausting clients, and success doesn't happen all the time. The emotional outbursts the PC absorbs minimize the ones the children must deal with. The PC must be humble, be brave, and call his/her colleagues frequently. The PC believes in principles and values and maintains, as an orienting beacon, those beliefs. An effective PC takes care of him/herself by being aware of what renews him/her and making time for these things.

COVERAGE

It is important to decide what, if any, kind of coverage you will provide for high-conflict clients when you are away from the office. Mental health professionals in particular tend to think that they should provide coverage, as they do for psychotherapy clients, but it is worth considering whether another professional can, in fact, take over a case even temporarily. A covering person does not have authority to arbitrate, nor is the covering professional familiar with the complex dynamics of a given family. On the other hand, sometimes a colleague with experience with high-conflict cases can provide some calming down of conflict and help clients wait until their PC is back at work. One author, a mental health professional, sends out a memo at least a month before a planned vacation informing PC clients about the vacation and offering to handle any issues that might be coming up before the break. The PC lets clients know that there will be no coverage during the vacation. The message on the PC's voice mail during the vacation time clearly specifies that coverage is provided for psychotherapy clients only and that the PC will return calls from PC clients upon returning to the office. Because high-conflict clients often also have other professionals involved with them—therapists and attorneys, for instance—the PC may wish to inform these professionals of any vacation, especially if the clients are likely to contact them in the PC's absence. As with many issues in PC work, there is no right or wrong way to handle coverage—one just needs to be clear with oneself and one's clients regarding what will be done.

TRANSFERENCE AND COUNTERTRANSFERENCE

Transference is one of the most complicated areas to navigate in working with high-conflict families. The struggles of these families are often heart wrenching, or infuriating, or both. The parents and children have extremely strong and often raw feelings about what has happened and is happening to them. They can evoke equally strong feelings in the professionals with whom they are involved. Frequently family members are so convinced of their own positions that they cannot entertain any other perspective on reality. Allegations of physical, emotional, and sexual abuse are common and are often difficult to rule in or rule out. Domestic violence is also a common occurrence in these families. The PC may be viewed as a possible savior, miracle worker, or as another ineffectual professional. There is fertile ground for very intense transference feelings on the part of the family members and equally strong reactions (countertransference) on the part of the PC.

It is helpful in managing these feelings for the PC to be clear on the stance he/she wants to take with the family. In being clear about the dynamics of the impasses and what the children need most from each parent, the PC's stance becomes the solid ground upon which to take a position (Johnston and Campbell 1988). The usual therapeutic neutrality and blankness may need to be replaced with a more direct and genuine response to set limits on the emotional outbursts from either parent.

A PC must be aware of his/her own countertransference feelings, because these may be a guide to understanding the experience of the children in the family. Examining these feelings will provide valuable clues about the family, the reactions they evoke in others, and most especially how the children experience the parents, their styles, and their conflicts. Colleagues familiar with the specific family or high conflict in general are invaluable resources for help in understanding and managing strong countertransference feelings.

HOW TO TERMINATE OR TRANSFER THE CASE

The original PC agreement should have a section specifying the terms for termination. The PC might feel that effective work is no longer occurring and elect to terminate his/her role or transfer it to another PC who has a different set of skills. On the other hand, the PC might feel that very effective work has been done and that it is time to phase out of the role of PC but to remain available to the parents as needed. One parent may refuse to continue participation in the parenting-coordination process and the PC must decide whether to terminate or consider another model of service for this family.

As a general rule, the original agreement should specify some period of time that provides a reasonable try at parenting coordination. This is typically at least six months and preferably a one- or two-year period. During this period, the PC cannot be fired or replaced by one parent alone unless ordered by the court. At the end of the specified period, the progress should be reviewed. Remember that progress is not necessarily based on how content either parent is with the process but, rather, on how well the children are doing emotionally and developmentally. The goal is to keep the children's exposure to the conflict minimized while allowing them to build as good a relationship as possible with each parent. If this goal has been met, then parenting coordination has been successful and the contract can be renewed. It may be that the parents are accepting more responsibility for managing their own communication and conflict containment, and the parenting coordinator may begin to phase out.

If there has been little progress or a stalemate, the PC should try to preserve whatever gains have been made yet acknowledge what has not worked. Consideration should be made of whether another PC would be advisable or whether this process is just not a workable model for this family. Not every case will meet with success, but most will have allowed the children to grow and mature free from the conflict for a period of time. The strength and increased coping that has come from this period of parenting coordination may well provide the children with a model of healthier conflict resolution and skills for self-growth.

Rules for a Successful Parenting Coordinator

1. Do not spread the conflict.
2. You, not the client, determine what constitutes an emergency.
3. You determine what information you need and from whom to perform your role.
4. Focus on the future, not the past.
5. Do not get aligned with one parent.
6. Do not use labels.
7. Always remain focused on the children.
8. Never inflict more damage to a family.
9. Do not waiver on decisions.
10. Read Chapter 18: Parting Thoughts, and take care of yourself.

Decisions, Dilemmas, Delights, Disasters

DEFINING YOUR ROLE CLEARLY

Susan, an emotionally fragile woman who shies away from people and becomes easily suspicious of others' motives, and Sam, her CEO ex-husband, agreed during their divorce settlement to use a Mediator-Arbitrator (Parenting Coordinator [PC] with arbitration power) to resolve any disputes regarding their son. They requested a preliminary interview with the PC when they were in the process of selecting which professional they would use for these services. Susan revealed that she had "fired" her attorney and did not intend to replace her. She asked the PC (who is a mental health professional) numerous questions about the PC's knowledge of the law and how the PC could possibly make decisions affecting her son without consulting an attorney or being familiar with the details of how the courts had decided similar issues. It seemed that Susan was interested in having legal expertise without retaining an attorney. She also seemed to be wondering if the PC had the ability to stand up to her ex-husband and his savvy attorney, who was still involved, if only peripherally.

The PC clearly and firmly clarified to Susan that the PC was not an attorney and that she would not consult an attorney every time a decision had to be arbitrated. The PC made sure Susan knew that a PC is not a substitute for an attorney who represents his/her client's interests. The PC spelled out the difference between taking a dispute to court, where the attorneys use the statutes and case law to argue their clients' cases and the judge is bound by the same in making the decision, and the PC process, where parents present their concerns and their views of what is in their child's best interest and the Med-Arbiter decides based on their presentations and what the Med-Arbiter believes is best. As a mental health professional, the PC has expertise in child development, divorce issues, and dispute resolution (not law) and would use this knowledge to help Susan and Sam make decisions when they could not do so themselves. The PC pointed out that the statutes covering arbitration specify how the process must be handled to ensure fairness, and emphasized what recourse Susan would have should she disagree with an arbitrated decision. Susan revealed her concern that the PC would be unduly swayed by Sam's attorney. The PC went over the details of how she and Sam would specify in the contract with whom the PC could communicate and gave examples of the kind of contact the PC usually has with attorneys. The PC also encouraged Susan and Sam to interview other PCs so that they could determine who they wanted to be making decisions for their son if they could not agree in the future. They did so and chose this PC. It took several tries before a wording acceptable to Susan was found that allowed the PC to communicate with Sam's attorney and his therapist. It was worth the time: the PC and the parents have as decent a working alliance as is possible with someone with Susan's level of suspiciousness and have survived the first major arbitration award that went against Susan's wishes.

WHEN ONE OF YOUR CLIENTS IS AN ATTORNEY

Randy, a 6-year-old boy, was constantly tugged at by his two very assertive parents. The mother was a highly contentious attorney and the father a strong advocate for father's rights. The PC agreement specified only mediation, not arbitration. The attorney mother would continually draw up arbitrated awards that favored her and increased her parenting time with her son. These would actually be drawn up in written form with a signature line provided for the PC, who was a psychologist, not an attorney. The mother would fax or mail these with the demand that they be immediately signed on the signature line and filed with the court.

Often she would come into the sessions with notes and memos, insisting that they be read before the process could begin. On one occasion, she laughingly said, "Well, it looks like you are going to have to have your own lawyer if you are going to continue to function as our PC. Isn't that true?"

Indeed, this was the ultimate solution to this case. The PC had the right in the agreement to resign and offer three names as replacement PCs. A resignation letter was filed with the court with three recommended professionals to assume the role. All three were attorneys with training in parenting coordination.

CONTAINING THE SPREAD OF THE CONFLICT

This case illustrates tribal warfare, which is a tactic often encountered in high-conflict divorce, as discussed in Chapter 3. Essentially, one parent enlists allies to his or her side of the conflict through networking. The details of the divorce and especially the atrocities committed by the other parent are spread far beyond the immediate family. The network might include the school, neighborhood, and recreational communities or go beyond this to the public media of newspaper and television. It often includes members of the parents' extended families, and professionals working with the family can also be drawn into the tribal warfare when they take sides excessively with one parent against the other.

The mother of a 14-year-old daughter had sole legal custody recommended by a custody evaluation and upheld by a court hearing. The father lived in a small prairie town in an adjoining state. He had very little visitation. Each time the daughter would go to visit him, there would be serious difficulty getting the daughter returned. The dad, when the daughter was with him, would take her to his church. The entire congregation would pray aloud for her to be placed into her father's custody and thus returned to the congregation.

The mother typically had to send the police to enforce the custody order and return the daughter. On one occasion, after the daughter was returned, the mother began to receive mail each day from the members of the father's church congregation. This was actually most of the town, which had a population of a few thousand. The mother's mailbox would be full of pleas from the members of the congregation to return the daughter to "where she belonged—her rightful place." Eventually the letters began to come directly to the daughter. Flyers announcing events in the church were sent initially, but over time the daughter received handwritten letters letting her know that her return and salvation were being prayed for.

The mother was obviously very upset. The father had a history of substance abuse and endangering behavior. Mother felt he had seriously distorted the truth to the members of his congregation.

The parenting coordinator had to make a decision regarding the ongoing visitation. It was decided that visitation to Dad's community was not in the daughter's best interest and consequently the dad's right to visitation had to be exercised in the community in which his daughter resided.

UNPAID BILLS FOR
PARENTING COORDINATION SERVICES

A common problem in parenting coordination services is un-paid bills, especially if the original agreement did not specify a retainer arrangement to draw against. In this case, the mother and father shared the costs of parenting coordination equally. Each was billed for one-half of the time each month. Each was consistently late with payment. Eventually, the amount due grew to be quite substantial. Both parents were informed that parenting-coordination services would have to be suspended until payment was received. The father did pay his share at this point but the mother did not. She was reminded repeatedly, and finally a check arrived. The check was for the full amount due and was sent by the pastor of the church. A letter accompanied the check stating that the church had taken such pity on this mother and her difficulties in the divorce situation that they were donating the collection plate from one specific service to pay her bill. The check, however, was not made out from the mother. The check was made out from the church to the PC. The PC was left with two dilemmas: (1) whether to cash this check and accept it as pay-ment, and (2) what to do about the letter, which made it quite clear that the church was praying for the mother. It was a persuasive letter designed to encourage the PC to take the mother's side.

After consultation with a colleague, the PC returned the check with a letter stating that it was a thoughtful and kind gesture of the church but that the preference of the PC would be that the church make the donation directly to the mother and then she could pay her own bill directly. The bill was never paid.

WHEN THE PARENTING COORDINATOR
LOSES CONTROL

High-conflict parents can argue incessantly. It becomes weari-some to listen to; eventually the patience of even the most sturdy of PCs wears thin. The PC's own emotions can be triggered as well as those of the clients.

After an extended period of listening to a mother and father bicker and pick at each other in an ever-rising crescendo, the PC started loudly clapping his hands and yelling, "Shut up! Be quiet!" His loud explosion got the parents' undivided attention and they did shut up. He apologized for his outburst but said he knew no other way to get their attention.

PCs work in a climate in which the clients easily become enraged. It would not be human to be unaffected by the rage. The artistry required of the PC is placing such conflict in context for the parents. When rageful behavior does happen, it is very important to stop whatever is being negotiated and insist that each person attempt to define what they saw as happening. Ways of preventing such an event from recurring need to be discussed. Setting some ground rules, such as no name calling and no interrupting, can be helpful. In this case, a "time out" procedure was established, which both parents continued to respect.

WHEN THE THERAPIST USURPS THE
PARENTING COORDINATOR ROLE

Therapists are often trained in roles other than psychotherapy. Staying within a defined role for a particular client is difficult for some therapists. In one specific case, the therapist for the mother also had a mediation practice. He felt that he knew many practical suggestions to resolve impasse issues for divorced parents. Gradu-ally, he shared more and more of his advice in this area, confusing his role. At one point, his suggestions ran directly counter to those of the PC.

The parents were experiencing difficulties with transitions. The PC recommended having the father deliver the children to the home of the mother rather than a pick-up system. This is often a helpful measure because it avoids the children waiting for a parent's arrival, having awkward moments in the doorway, and arguing about lateness in front of the children. The therapist, however, had recommended that the mother continue to pick up the children and have sanctions imposed for lateness. The mother felt the suggestion of her therapist was the one to be followed whereas the father accepted the suggestion of the PC. A difficult issue grew more conflictual as a result of the unclear roles. Communication between the PC and therapist is essential if the PC senses that role boundaries are not being respected.

WHEN INSIGHT BACKFIRES

Early in our experiences as PCs, two of the authors worked together on a high-conflict case that had already had numerous professionals (therapists and custody evaluators) involved. The parents were continuing battles that had begun prior to their separation and had abated only minimally and temporarily since their final orders. Both parents had remarried, and the new spouses, although not actively involved in perpetuating the conflict, were at least passively supportive of their current spouses. The authors formulated a comprehensive understanding of the dynamics between the parents and what each did that provoked the other's negative responses. The parents were offered an opportunity to work with one PC to try to mediate their disputes about parenting time and schools, while the other PC waited in the wings to be an arbitrator if need be—a way of bifurcating roles that we wanted to try out. One of the authors then attempted to work with each parent individually toward this goal.

It included trying to help them gain insight into what set off the other parent and so know how to avoid this if they so chose. Because the parents had spent several tens of thousands of dollars on professionals already to no avail, they were willing to try this approach. It failed abysmally—one parent took the information and proceeded to push every button the PC had identified as something that would drive the other parent crazy. The conflict escalated; the PC stopped the attempt to use insight with these parents and to mediate the disputes, and the other PC took over as arbitrator. We learned then that sometimes what people benefit most from the PC is simply someone to make decisions, not to try to impart insight or change behavior.

CONTAINING THE CONFLICT BY CONSTRUCTING A NETWORK OF PROFESSIONALS

Two parents who were disagreeing about how their children would spend time with both of them were assigned one of the authors as a Special Advocate to make recommendations to the Court. The parents decided to accept the Special Advocate's recommendations and requested that the Special Advocate remain involved with them and have arbitration power in some specific areas in order to preclude any more costly court battles. Their attorneys drafted a stipulation to that effect.

The younger child in this family was sorely in need of therapy to gain confidence in listening to her own voices and lessen her anxious attempts to keep both parents happy. Because previous attempts at therapy had become inextricably intertwined with the parental conflicts, the therapy was carefully set up so that both parents agreed upon who would see the child. Each parent would have limited contact with the therapist, but the therapist would be able to involve either parent in sessions as therapeutically indicated for the child's sake, and notify the Special Advocate of any concerns needing intervention. In addition, each parent would have an individual therapist available, and the Special Advocate could have access to any or all of the therapists if a decision had to be made. If need be, the Special Advocate could talk with the child directly, but everyone agreed to try to avoid this.

The Special Advocate usually met with the parents separately, and then proposals were put into writing with each parent having an opportunity to respond to the other's proposals. The parents thus did not have much direct contact with each other and the child was given the breathing room necessary to develop a solid identity separate from the pressures of the parents. The Special Advocate got needed information to assist in decision making, but the child did not have to be involved in the minutiae of the parental conflict, which in the past had caused so many attempts to please. Although the structure was complicated, it succeeded in de-escalating the conflict and providing a layer or two of insulation around the child. This has proved to promote healthy growth for the child and more effective decision making for the parents.

CONFRONTING WITH COMPASSION AND FIRMNESS

One PC client who had numerous serious mental health problems and an alcohol problem occasionally raged at the PC when things did not go his way. He took his daughter on a vacation and had negotiated with the girl's mother, through the PC, that the usual parenting time schedule would be shifted forward a few days to accommodate the trip. The girl was then due to go back to her mom's the day after returning from the trip. The PC got an urgent call from the dad that day, after the girl had returned to her mother's home, insisting that the PC call the mom and have her return the girl to the father that evening because he "wasn't ready for her to be gone" and was feeling bereft without his daughter.

The PC refused, reminding the dad of his agreement about

the schedule change and also stating that it was not the daughter's job to take care of his feelings. He said, "Yes, it is," became enraged, hung up on the PC, and then left several angry voice-mail messages saying the PC was like everyone else and expected him to act like a robot with no feelings. He indicated that he had did not want to talk to the PC ever again. The PC responded by writing a letter to the dad, reminding him firmly of some events in their past experiences when the PC had most definitely "allowed" him "to have feelings." The PC also reiterated her stance that it is not the daughter's job to take care of her parent's feelings, that this was damaging to her. She deserves to have her needs met, not be asked to meet her father's. This was coupled with the PC's perception that the dad loved his daughter and acted in her behalf much of the time, but at times was overwhelmed by his own pain and couldn't at those moments think of what is best for her. The PC clearly stated that the dad deserved comfort for his own pain; however, this should not come from the daughter but from the dad's friends and therapist. The PC acknowledged the dad's right to discontinue working together (as their contract allowed) and indicated she would be willing to continue if the dad so chose as long as the dad understood the PC would continue to call things as she saw them.

A few days later the dad left the PC a voice mail thanking her for the "nice note." It was not a letter most people would describe as "nice." The dad was used to people distancing from him when he erupted with rage, and so to him having someone hang in there with him when he was angry, set limits on his unhealthy behavior, and yet still show some compassion for the pain underneath his acting out and some respect for his parenting was indeed "nice." The PC was not "fired" at that point.

THE CASE OF TOO MANY FATHERS

The PC must carefully consider who to include in the parenting-coordination process at the beginning as well as at various

junctures along the way. The following case was highly complicated because of the number of fathers. The mother had a child
with another man, which she covered up for several years. This
son was brought up in a family that had children from a previous
marriage who visited with the mother's ex-husband. The boy grew
up believing that the father of his brothers was his father, but he
was not. The secret was revealed when the biological father of the
boy filed for paternity and was granted the right to visitation. The
boy, however, already had a full family life with his brothers and
their father. Numerous issues had to be sorted out. Was it best for
him to continue visitation with the father of his brothers, to whom
he was now bonded? Was visitation with two fathers within the
realm of reasonableness and possible from a time-sharing point
of view? Would both fathers be included in the parenting-
coordination process, together or individually?

What eventually worked was a surprise to the PC. The son was
clearly bonded to the father of his brothers, and he strongly
wished to continue his visitation with him. The ex-husband
respected the right of the biological father to also form a
relationship with his son and was willing to share the visitation
time. Eventually both fathers and the mother participated in the
parenting-coordination sessions, working toward a reasonable
time-sharing schedule. The arrangement worked for many years.
The son had two identified fathers and one mother, all of whom
lived in separate homes. This boy counted himself fortunate,
stating that he felt very loved and nurtured by them all. Amaz-
ingly, some cases have surprising and happy resolutions.

DIVORCE IS NOT THE END OF THE WORLD:
MORE EXTREME LIFE CIRCUMSTANCES

The job of the parenting coordinator often includes putting the
high-conflict impasse into a perspective in which the parents can
more effectively deal with it. One poignant example comes to

mind. A highly contentious couple were fighting over every aspect of parenting time for their 4-year-old daughter. They were truly acting out the divorce conflict, their anger with each other, their mistrust, and their hurt—all to an extreme. Sadly, reality dealt a serious blow to this couple when the father was diagnosed with cancer. He was at a fairly advanced stage by the time the diagnosis came back, and it was evident that he was going to need intensive surgery in addition to chemotherapy. All family members realized that the father might die.

As a result of the tragedy, this couple pulled together and came to their senses. They came into the PC's office and looked at each other and talked about their needs for each other, their respect for each other, the fact that their child needed both of them involved in her life. They decided at that point that they were going to bury their hatchets and from that point forward they would pull together, and support her in terms of having two parents. Faced with such a serious life crisis, the parents were able to put into perspective the fact that this divorce and separation were not the worst thing that ever happened to them. They realized that they could be dealt much more serious blows.

It has been about three years since this occurred, and dad is doing very well; his cancer is in remission. Interestingly, this couple has never returned for parenting coordination. In chance encounters with the dad in the community, he has informed the PC that the couple continues to get along well, they no longer have issues of parenting time, and that their child is thriving in a relationship with both parents. The Chinese proverb is right: "Crisis entails both danger and opportunity."

If there were a way to create this awareness artificially, without having to face such a serious crisis, maybe many other couples could benefit. Putting divorce into a context and educating through the experience of others may help bickering, angry couples to compartmentalize their conflict and get on with the task of parenting.

In another family with intense divorce conflict, the professional serving as the PC lost her own daughter in a tragic and sudden death. The divorced father, who often raged at the PC in an effort to gain more time with his own daughter, gained a new perspective and appreciation for the time he did have with his daughter. He wrote a lovely condolence letter apologizing for his intimidating behavior and agreed to attend parenting classes, which he previously refused, insisting he was an exemplary father who needed no guidance.

Putting divorce, as painful as it is, into a larger context of more profound loss helps some couples to contain their conflict, curb their bickering, and appreciate the specialness of being a parent at all, married or divorced. Creating this awareness through developing empathy for the pain of others without personally being faced with such a serious crisis evokes insight for some couples.

PRESERVING THE PARENT–CHILD RELATIONSHIP

Allegations of abuse can trigger a windfall of escalating emotions that gravely impair trust and any possibility of a normalized parenting time schedule. Regardless of whether the allegations are founded, one parent is likely to endlessly feel misgivings about the child's safety with the other parent. Supervised parenting time is typically the first step in such situations, but eventually efforts to move toward unsupervised and more normalized parenting time need to be made. Unable to trust, the fearful parent may be able to manage his or her anxious feelings if rapport has been established with a PC who will keep a careful and guarded eye on the child's well-being.

One parenting coordinator in the Denver area had such a case where a 6-year-old girl made allegations that her father had sexually abused her during a two-week-long out-of-state summer visitation. The court intervened and appointed a PC to plan the time-sharing schedule. Having a PC has kept this relationship, which would have definitely fallen by the wayside, alive. The PC arranged a time-sharing schedule for the little girl that began with the father traveling to the city where his daughter lived. Initially, he had supervised visitation, which moved to a phase of going out into the world with a trusted adult, and then into the world alone with "debriefing sessions," which allowed the child to meet following each visit with a professional who documented her feelings about each visit.

The PC made the overarching plans, saw that each phase was implemented, and that everyone's needs were met. The little girl felt protected and safe while the father had a means to continue his visitation. Over the course of approximately two years the relationship healed enormously. This would have been an impossible situation to handle at a distance, and there probably would have been a loss of a father in this child's life had the court not had the wisdom to appoint a PC.

Chapter 14 specifies possible steps for moving from supervised phases of visitation into unsupervised phases. Chapter 13 offers guidelines developed by a highly competent group of attorneys, mental health professionals, and judges to guide courts in deciding when supervised visitation may be necessary for the protection of a child. Unlike other guidelines, these offer levels of supervision based on the seriousness of the safety concerns, both physical and emotional.

WHEN THE PARENTING COORDINATOR MAKES A MISTAKE

High-conflict situations are very difficult and every PC will make some mistakes. We have found it helpful to be straightforward with our clients and to admit our errors. This approach has several benefits:

- Parents are shown by example how one can admit a mistake, make appropriate corrections, and move on. This can be very important learning for parents who are not able to admit their own mistakes or to handle their ex-spouses' mistakes.
- The PC gets valuable information about the parents by observing how they handle the situation. Often the parents' true colors come shining through in their behavior around the PC's mistake.
- Parents may get a more realistic view of the PC as a person who can be helpful but who is not perfect or infallible. Frequently, parents in high conflict have unrealistically high expectations of themselves or others.
- The parents may have increased respect for the PC—it takes courage to admit an error and correct it.

The PC should be careful not to retreat from being firm and decisive in the wake of a mistake.

Leo, a teenage boy, did not like visiting his mother. His parents came to the PC because they could not agree about how much time Leo should spend with his mother. The mother wanted more time than the father was comfortable with. Father was quite upset about Leo's discomfort with his mother and wished Leo didn't have to go unless he wanted to. Mother was quite insistent about her rights to see her son and frequently initiated legal action to gain access to him.

The PC was asked to help the parents negotiate a schedule for a specific weekend and was successful in getting an agreement. Because of restraining orders in place, the PC did not meet with the parents together but instead used "shuttle diplomacy." After the father agreed to a schedule acceptable to the mother, which lessened her time by a few hours, the PC neglected to call the mother and tell her that the shortened hours would be in effect. The PC simply forgot to call. In addition, the parenting coordinator was perhaps taking for granted that the mother would know that the father would jump at her willingness to shorten the visit by a few hours.

During the weekend, Leo said something to his mother about his father picking him up at three o'clock instead of 6:00 P.M. and mother disagreed. Leo even called his father to confirm the time and was told he was right. Mother, however, persisted, and planned to take Leo to a movie that started at 2:30 P.M. When Leo again called his father, he was told to go with the mother as it was not worth the possible fallout to fight about it.

The PC heard about the confusion the next Monday. Each parent's behavior over the weekend added valuable information to the PC's assessment of the family. The father had been quite passive and had not been willing to stand up to the mother on Leo's behalf. The mother had taken advantage of the confusion to grab more time with Leo but at the expense of damaging her relationship with him. The PC called each parent and discussed their reactions, what they did that was not in Leo's best interest, and how they could have been more helpful to their son. The PC also wrote a letter to both parents detailing the error and apologizing for it. She also made it very clear that in the future the parents should call her rather than allow the situation to continue. Because Leo was right that he was supposed to return to his father's early, the PC supported an early return the next weekend. The PC called Leo on the phone to explain and apologize to him in person. The parents were appreciative of the apology but also clearly received a message that each in their own way had not acted in Leo's best interest.

WHEN NO NEWS IS GOOD NEWS

A high-conflict couple followed the recommendation of their custody evaluators and arranged to have a PC with arbitration powers available to assist them after their divorce was final. At first, sessions were extremely tense and they could not agree on much of anything. Even when they had input from the children's therapist about their needs, the fight between the parents took precedence and precluded resolution without the PC's intervention. Eventually, they needed the PC primarily to assist in setting the summer parenting schedule. Their final orders laid out the guidelines for how the children should divide their summer vacation between mom and dad, but each year, the details had to be worked out.

In the winter, at the annual meeting with the PC to decide the summer schedule, one parent made a request for a significant change in how the time would be divided. The change would not alter the annual percentage of time each parent had with the children, but would redistribute it in a way that would radically change how the summer was handled. The parents could not agree on either the specifics of the schedule or the need for the change. They decided to consult the therapist who had helped the children during the height of the family's conflict and whom they both trusted. The parents sent proposals to each other and the PC, and the therapist sent a letter to both parents and the PC after seeing the children. The PC never got the expected call to schedule another session. In an unrelated contact with the therapist, the PC found out that the parents had been able to focus on the children's needs as articulated by the therapist, put aside the old inclination to fight with one another, and decide the schedule themselves.

Part IV

Case-Management Guidelines

10

Parenting Plan for High Conflict

High-conflict families benefit from a very structured plan that details the drop-off and pick-up dates with times and locations. Holiday plans, similarly, must be specific, as well as attendance at events and means of communication. The goal of a parenting plan for a high-conflict family is disengagement between the parents with access between the children and each parent. Parallel parenting techniques that minimize contact and conflict are paramount in designing these plans.

FORM 10–1:
PLAN FOR A HIGH-CONFLICT COUPLE
(School-age children)

1. **The parties have joint custody and have agreed to work with
   _____(professional's name)_____ as a PC with mediation-
   arbitration powers.**

2. **During the school year, as defined by the school calendar, the
   children will reside with the mother.**

3. **During the school year, the children will spend time with the
   father as follows:**

   a) *Every other weekend,* from Friday when the father or his
   appointee will pick the children up from school, until Monday
   morning when the father or his appointee will return the
   children to school.

   b) *During the week* when the weekend is a visiting weekend with the mother, the father shall have the children for a
   Wednesday night visit. The visit will begin immediately after
   school (school day care may be used if pick up cannot be
   immediate). The children will be returned to school on
   Thursday morning.

   c) *Every fourth week* when the children will be with the
   mother on the weekend, the father shall have the female child
   on Tuesday from after school until the following morning when
   the child will be returned to school. On Thursday of that week,
   the father shall have the male child from after school until the
   following morning when he will be returned to school. As
   above, day care and pick up by an appointee may be followed
   if needed.

4. **School breaks will be handled as follows:**

   a) *Christmas Vacation*

The vacation will be divided in half, to include the use of a half day if necessary. The shift between households will occur at 12:00 P.M. (noon) on the appropriate day.

Father shall have the first half of Christmas Vacation in even-numbered years, mother in odd-numbered ones.

Christmas and Christmas Eve days shall be observed as follows: The parent in whose section of the vacation Christmas falls shall observe Christmas with the children. The parent who does not observe Christmas shall have the children from 8:00 A.M. to 8:00 P.M. on Christmas Eve day.

On those years when mother does not have the second half of the Christmas vacation, father will return the children on New Year's Day at 6:00 P.M.

b) *Spring Break*

Spring break shall be alternated each year, with father observing it with the children in even-numbered years, mother in odd-numbered ones.

Spring break will begin immediately after school on Friday. The children will be picked up by the parent who has them that year.

The children will be returned to school by the spring break parent the following Monday.

c) *Summer Vacation*

The summer vacation will be divided in half. It will begin three (3) days after the close of school and end five (5) days before the opening of school. Father shall have the first half of summer vacataion in even-numbered years, mother in odd-numbered years.

If away-from-home vacations occur during either parent's half, they are obligated to inform the other parent as to the destination, travel route, and/or ticket information within ten (10) days prior to the departure. These will also be filed with the Mediator-Arbitrator who will, at all times, hold the children's passports until an appropriate release time.

When the children are simply at home, they will visit with the other parent one day per week, to include an overnight. The children, wherever possible, will be picked up from day camp and returned to day camp the following morning. If this is not possible, they will negotiate a comfortable, neutral pick up and drop off with the final approval of the Mediator-Arbitrator. If the children are on a vacation trip, those days, of course will not be observed.

5. Holidays and birthdays will be handled as follows:

a) *Mother's Day*

Regardless of their normal visitation schedule, the children will spend Mother's Day Sunday from 9:00 A.M. to 8:00 P.M. with their mother.

b) *Father's Day*

Regardless of their normal visitation schedule, the children will spend Father's Day Sunday with their father from 9:00 A.M. to 8:00 P.M.

c) *Thanksgiving Weekend*

The weekend will begin immediately after school on Wednesday and end at 8:00 P.M. on Sunday.

The weekend will alternate with spring break, so mother will observe it with the children in even-numbered years.

d) *New Year's Eve and Day*

These days will be observed by the parent with whom the children are during the second half of the Christmas vacation.

e) *Easter Sunday*

Easter Sunday will be alternated each year, with father observing it with the children in odd-numbered years, mother in even-numbered years. It will begin at 6:00 P.M. Saturday night and end at 6:00 P.M. Sunday night.

f) *Memorial Day Weekend*

Memorial Day weekend will begin immediately after school on Friday and end on Tuesday morning after Memorial Day. Its observance will override the regular visitation schedule. It will be celebrated with father in odd-numbered years, mother in even-numbered years.

g) *Labor Day Weekend*

This weekend will begin immediately after school on Friday and end Tuesday morning when the children are returned to school. Father will observe the weekend with the children in odd-numbered years, mother in even-numbered years.

h) *July 4th*

The day will begin at 9:00 A.M. on the Fourth and end at 10:00 A.M. on July 5th, where the children will be returned to the appropriate parent.

i) *Father's and Mother's Birthdays*

Parents' birthdays will always transcend the regular visitation schedule. If either parent's birthday is during the school year, observation will begin immediately after school on school days and end at 8:00 P.M.. On non-school days, the observation will begin at noon and end at 8:00 P.M..

j) *Children's Birthdays*

The children's birthdays will be observed with the parent with whom they reside when the birthday falls. The other parent will make alternative plans to celebrate the children's birthdays when the children are with them according to the normal co-parenting schedule.

6. Out-of-Town Travel

If a parent must be out of town for fewer than forty-nine (49) hours, they are responsible for arranging child care for the children. If they are going to be gone three days or more, then the other parent must be offered first right of refusal. If that parent cannot care for the children, it is up to the traveling parent to arrange full-time child care until their return. If a parent accepts care of the children, there will be no make-up time for the absent parent.

7. Telephone Access

The children may call the other parent whenever they like for up to two telephone calls a day.

The parent may call the children once per every forty-eight (48) hours of absence. Children are to be given privacy for their telephone conversations by the residential parent. The call is to be placed at a mutually agreed upon time, mediated if necessary, which will remain the same over the weeks. The residential parent is obligated to ensure the presence of the children and the absence of any activity that may draw them away from a phone call (i.e., favorite TV program, neighborhood outdoor activity a block away).

8. Transportation

The basic principle is that the parent having the child is responsible to deliver the child to the parent who is supposed to have the child or to the event or activity the child is to attend.

9. Mediation-Arbitration Decision Making

Education, health care, child care, religious training, and operation of a motor vehicle issues always will be referred for mediation-arbitration. All such decisions must be made jointly or arbitrated. They may not be made unilaterally.

Also, decisions that impact on the other parent in terms of time commitments, finances, or transportation shall be made jointly with the assistance of Mediator-Arbitrator if necessary.

10. Communication

All communications about the children shall be written in a communication book that shall pass with the children as they pass between households. In it are to be noted important events of the previous week, the children's health and need for current medication, and upcoming appointments that may affect the children's scheduling. Requests for parenting times may also be entered. Silence in regard to a request shall be considered a "yes". The book may not be used to note or criticize either parent's behavior.

11. Day-to-Day Decisions

Decisions about bedtime, hygiene, minor disciplinary actions, minor medical and dental procedures, curfew, chores, allowances, social dress, and jewelry shall be the province of the household in which the child dwells at the moment.

12. Emergencies

Each parent is required to notify the other parent within three (3) hours of any medical emergency. The parent present is authorized to sign legal consents for both parents to permit emergency intervention.

13. Information

Each parent is required to set up their own information network for information about school and routine medical appointments. Each is required to tell professionals that they hold joint custody, and each parent has equal rights to access information. On any emergency information sheet, each parent will list the other as the first person to contact if he or she is not reachable.

14. Geographical Relocation

Relocation within the Denver metropolitan area (Jefferson, Adams, Boulder, Denver, Douglas, and Arapaho counties) may be done only after med-arb has taken place as to the required changes in the children's schooling, day care, and after-school activities. The children may not be removed permanently from Colorado without the express approval of the other parent or a mediation-arbitration decision.

15. Review of Agreement

During the month of June each year, the custody recommendations shall be reviewed and modified as agreed through mediation.

16. Mediation-Arbitration

Mediation-arbitration shall be used whenever an impasse is reached. At the time of final orders, a Mediator-Arbitrator shall be selected by the parents or appointed by the court.

Note: The examples above are not exhaustive in terms of recommendations. They are intended to offer the range of issues that must be covered and the depth of detail in which recommendations must be addressed.

11

Parenting-Coordinator Agreement

Parenting Coordinators (PCs) should always specify the scope of their arbitration authority in their agreements. Whether or not confidentiality will be maintained should also be specified.

Form 11–1 is a PC agreement with limited mediation-arbitration.

Form 11–2 consists of confidentiality clauses.

FORM 11–1:
PARENTING-COORDINATOR AGREEMENT
WITH ARBITRATION LIMITED TO SPECIFIED AREAS

We, _____ and _____ hereby appoint
____(professional's name)____ to function as Parenting Coordinator.

1. **Parenting Coordination:** We understand that the function of a
   Parenting Coordinator (PC) is to help parents resolve their
   differences regarding their child(ren) and their care in a
   manner that serves the best interests of the child(ren), minimizes conflict between parents that could harm the child(ren),
   and fosters cooperation between parents. The PC may assess
   the situation and educate us as necessary regarding child
   development and communication and facilitate communication between us and with others involved with our child(ren).
   The PC may also mediate disputes between us, coach on
   strategies of dealing with the other parent and with the
   child(ren), and may refer us to other professionals, such as
   therapists. We specifically give the PC the authority to arbitrate
   the following types of decisions:

   a) _____

   b) _____

   c) _____

   d) _____

2. **Mediation:** The PC is a trained and experienced mediator. As
   PC, he (she) may mediate between the parents as necessary,
   that is, help the parents to make their own decisions, but his
   (her) role is not exclusively as a mediator.

   a) In mediation, all written and oral communications,
   negotiations, and statements made in the course of mediation
   are considered confidential. However, because information

provided in mediation shall be considered by the PC in making an arbitration award, confidentiality is not insured.

b) It is understood that the PC may disclose the following information: (1) he (she) has reason to believe that a child is in need of protection, (2) either parent is in danger of bodily harm, or (3) he (she) learns of the intent to commit a felony.

3. **Legal Advice:** The PC does not offer legal advice, nor does he (she) provide legal counsel. Each parent is advised to retain his/her own attorney in order to be properly counseled about his/her legal interests, rights, and responsibilities.

4. **Process of Arbitration:**

a) It is our intent to resolve issues through mediation as much as possible. In the event that we are unable to reach a mutually satisfactory resolution of a dispute, we ask that __(professional's name)__ serve as arbitrator and arbitrate the issue and make a decision for us based upon the communication and information that we have provided. In addition, the PC and/or either of us may also request the submission of written statements of position and facts to the PC. Either of us may then respond in writing to the other parent's statement. The PC shall then review the statements and responses and issue a written arbitration award regarding the issue. We understand and agree that we will be bound by the award of the PC, who is acting as an arbitrator subject to the provisions of C.R.S. 14-10-128.5 ___(or other state statute)___ .

b) We agree that either of us may request that an arbitration hearing be held. In the event of a formal arbitration hearing, the following procedure shall be followed:

(1) One week prior to hearing on the matters to be submitted to arbitration, or at such other time as designated by the PC, each parent shall submit a

statement to the PC that shall summarize the matters in dispute; the legal issues pending; the legal authority supporting his/her position, if appropriate; the witnesses who shall testify; and a brief summary of each witness's testimony.

(2) The parents may stipulate to the PC consulting with expert witnesses, such as therapists, custody evaluators, etc., outside of the hearing and may agree that such information received may be considered by the PC in the Award.

(3) The hearing date and time shall be determined by mutual agreement of the parties. Notice of the hearing shall be by U.S. mail, postage prepaid. The PC, in his (her) sole discretion, may grant a continuance of the hearing upon request of either parent for good cause or by stipulation of the parents. All hearings shall be held at the offices of the PC unless the parties and PC agree otherwise.

(4) Either parent may provide a certified court reporter for all arbitration hearing proceedings and shall be responsible for all expenses associated with a record of the proceedings.

5. **Law:** We agree to be bound by the Colorado Uniform Arbitration Act, C.R.S. 13-22 201, et seq. and the Uniform Dissolution of Marriage Act, C.R.S. 14-10-101, et seq. _____(or other state statutes)____.

6. **Telephone Conferences:** Telephone conferences will be available upon request.

7. **Communication:** Copies of all correspondence to the PC must be mailed, faxed, emailed, or hand delivered to the other parent with a "cc:" notated on the correspondence unless otherwise directed by the PC.

8. **Appointments:** Appointments with the PC shall be scheduled at the request of either of us by phone or in person with no written notice required unless we have a court order that provides a different process. We agree to make a good-faith effort to be available for appointments when requested by the other parent or the PC.

9. **Involvement of PC in Litigation:**

   a) We agree not to request, subpoena, or demand the production of any record, notes, work product, or the like of the PC concerning his (her) work with us. To the extent that we may have a right to demand these documents, that right is hereby waived.

   b) We agree that the PC shall not be called as a witness in any subsequent proceeding unless required by statute or court order.

10. **Witnesses:** We stipulate to the PC consulting with professionals and others who have information about us or our child(ren), such as therapists, custody evaluators, schoolteachers, etc., and agree that such information received may be considered by the PC in entering an arbitration award.

11. **Fees:**

   a) We agree to pay the PC for all of his (her) time and costs in working with us, including time spent by the PC reviewing documents and correspondence; meeting with us; phone conferences with us, our attorneys, professionals, and others; and deliberation and issuance of arbitration awards, at the rate of $ _____ per hour. We also agree to pay the costs incurred by the PC, including but not limited to long-distance telephone calls, copies, fax charges, etc.

   b) We shall pay the PC's fees and costs in the following manner: _____ shall pay _____ % and _____ shall pay _____ %. We understand that in the event we must reschedule or cancel an appointment, unless we notify the PC more than forty-eight (48) hours prior to the scheduled appointment, we will be billed for one hour of the PC's time. In the event that one of us does not appear for a scheduled appointment and has not given 48-hours advance notice and the other parent does appear or is prepared to appear, the parent who does not appear shall be responsible for both parents' fees. Nonpayment of fees shall be grounds for the resignation of the PC. We each shall deposit with the PC a retainer of $ _____ upon the signing of this Agreement. The PC shall only be entitled to any or all of the retainer as he (she) spends time on our case. We will replenish the retainer to the level of $ _____ per parent upon its depletion.

12. **Award:** When the PC makes decisions for us (arbitrates), the PC shall issue an award in writing and deliver a copy of said award to each of us and to his or her respective attorney by U.S. mail, postage prepaid, within fourteen (14) days, or at a later date as circumstances may control, from the date of the completion of the arbitration process. The PC's final award shall be binding upon both parents pursuant to C.R.S. 14-10-128.5 _____ (or other state statute)_____ and shall be filed by the PC with the District Court to be confirmed by the District Court in accordance with Section 13-22-213 C.R.S. _____ (or other state statute)_____ .

13. **Correction:** In most cases, the PC will provide the parents with a draft award prior to filing the award with the court. Any request for correction or modification of an award by the PC pursuant to Section 13-22-215 C.R.S. _____ (or other state statute)_____ shall be directed to the PC first rather than to the District Court within seven (7) days of the award.

14. **Interviewing Children:** The PC is authorized to interview our child(ren) privately in order to ascertain the child's needs as to

the issues being arbitrated. In conducting such an interview, the PC shall avoid forcing the child to choose between us.

15. **Time:** The PC is authorized to tell either or both of us if he (she) believes that an inordinate amount of time is being taken by either or both of us in this process. We agree that the amount of time spent on resolving a dispute be in proportion to the nature of the dispute, as determined by the PC.

16. **Term:** The term of the PC's service shall be a period of _____ months from the date of execution of this Agreement (from the later date if signed by us on different dates). At the end of the term, if one of us and/or the PC desires to terminate the professional relationship with the PC, this Agreement shall be terminated. The service of the PC may be terminated prior to the end of the term if we both agree that we wish to terminate the PC's service or if the PC requests to withdraw prior to the termination date.

17. **Other Agreements:**

_____

Client

_____

Client

_____

Parenting Coordinator

Signed this _____ day of _____ , _____ .

FORM 11–2:
CONFIDENTIALITY CLAUSES

Consent to Confidentiality

All communications, observations, and opinions derived from contact with the Parenting Coordinator (PC) shall be considered confidential. The parties agree that neither of them nor anyone representing either party, in any capacity, or acting as an agent for either party, shall call upon the PC at any time to provide either written reports or oral testimony at any deposition, court hearing, or trial on any issue related to or arising out of the role of the PC.

Neither party shall subpoena any records of the PC for any purpose including, but not limited to, use as evidence at any court or other proceedings. It is understood that the PC is acting as a psychotherapist and is required by law to report suspicion of child abuse or endangerment to self and others to Social Services or the police.

Therefore, each party waives any right either of them may have to call any person or subpoena any record in any dissolution or child custody or visitation action that is or may be filed.

Consent to Nonconfidentiality

The parties agree and understand that no communication between the parents or children and the PC are confidential and such communications will be admissible in evidence if the PC is called as a witness.

12

Mediation-Arbitration Agreement

In most states both parents must consent to arbitration of parenting issues. State laws govern the binding/nonbinding nature of arbitration awards. Typically, the Med-Arbiter remains available on an ongoing basis as parenting issues arise.

FORM 12–1:
MEDIATION-ARBITRATION AGREEMENT

We, _____ and _____
hereby appoint ____(professional's name)____ to function as Med-
Arbiter of disagreements about the following types of decisions regarding our child(ren):

1. **Med-Arb:** We understand that mediation-arbitration (med-arb)
   is a process of alternative dispute resolution that begins as
   assisted negotiations and becomes arbitration in which a binding decision is made by the Med-Arbiter only if we are unable
   to resolve our dispute in the mediation process.

2. **Mediation:**

   a) In mediation all written and oral communications,
   negotiations, and statements made in the course of mediation
   are considered confidential. However, because information
   provided in mediation shall be considered by the Med-Arbiter
   in making an arbitration issue, confidentiality is not insured in
   mediation arbitration.

   b) The mediator does not offer legal advice, nor does he
   (she) provide legal counsel. Each party is advised to retain
   his/her own attorney in order to be properly counseled about
   his/her legal interests, rights, and obligations.

   c) It is understood that the mediator may disclose the
   following information: (1) if he (she) has reason to believe that
   a child is in need of protection; (2) that either party is in
   danger of bodily harm; or (3) if he (she) learns of the intent to
   commit a felony.

   d) It is understood that full disclosure of all relevant and
   pertinent information is essential to the mediation process.
   Accordingly, there will be a complete and honest disclosure by
   each of the parties to the other and to the mediator of all
   relevant information and documents. This includes providing

each other and the mediator with all information and documentation that would usually be available through the discovery process in a legal proceeding. If either party fails to make such full disclosure, then the agreement reached in mediation may be set aside.

3. Process of Med-Arb:

a) It is our intent to resolve our issues ourselves through mediation. In the event that we are unable to reach a mutually satisfactory resolution of the dispute, we ask that _____ (Med-Arbiter's name) _____ arbitrate the issue and make a decision for us based upon the disclosures that were made in the mediation process. In addition, the Med-Arbiter and/or either of us may also request the submission of written statements of position and facts to the Med-Arbiter. Either of us may then respond in writing to the other party's statement. The Med-Arbiter shall then review the statements and responses and issue a written Arbitration Award regarding the issue. We understand and agree that we will be bound by the Award of the Med-Arbiter appointed by us herein subject to the provisions of C.R.S. 14-10-128.5.1 _____ (or other state statute) _____ .

b) We agree that either of us after mediating an issue may request that an arbitration hearing be held. In the event of a formal arbitration hearing, the following procedure shall be followed:

(1) One week prior to a hearing on the matters to be submitted to arbitration, or at such other time as designated by the Med-Arbiter, each party shall submit a statement to the Med-Arbiter that shall summarize the matters in dispute, the legal issues pending, the legal authority supporting his or her position, if appropriate; the witnesses who shall testify; and a brief summary of each witness's testimony.

(2) The parties may stipulate to the Med-Arbiter consulting with expert witnesses, such as therapists,

custody evaluators, etc., outside of the hearing and may agree that such information received may be considered by the Med-Arbiter in the Award.

(3) The hearing date and time shall be determined by mutual agreement of the parties. Notice of the hearing shall be by U.S. mail, postage prepaid. The Med-Arbiter, in his/her sole discretion, may grant a continuance of the hearing upon request of either party for good cause or by stipulation of the parties. All hearings shall be held at the offices of the Med-Arbiter unless the parties and Med-Arbiter agree otherwise.

(4) Either party may provide a certified court reporter for all arbitration hearing proceedings and shall be responsible for all expenses associated with a record of the proceedings.

4. **Law:** We agree to be bound by the Colorado Uniform Arbitration Act, C.R.S. 13-22 201, et seq. and the Uniform Dissolution of Marriage Act, C.R.S. 14-10-101, et seq. _____ (or other state statutes). (A copy of this statute is attached.)

5. **Telephone Conferences:** Telephone conference mediation-arbitration sessions will be available upon request.

6. **Communication:** Copies of all correspondence to the Med-Arbiter must be mailed, faxed, emailed, or hand delivered to the other party with a "cc:" notated on the correspondence.

7. **Appointments:** Appointments for mediation-arbitration shall be scheduled at the request of either of us by phone or in person with no written notice required unless we have a court order that provides a different process. We agree to make a good-faith effort to be available for mediation-arbitration conferences when requested by the other party or the Med-Arbiter.

8. **Financial Disclosure:** If economic issues are involved, each party shall at the direction of the Med-Arbiter exchange and

file with the Med-Arbiter, prior to the mediation-arbitration session, a full and complete Affidavit as to Financial Affairs and shall update said affidavit as may be necessary, unless otherwise agreed upon by the parties. Corruption, fraud, misconduct, or the submission of false or misleading financial information, documents, or evidence by a party shall be grounds for an application to the court to vacate any award issued pursuant to this Agreement.

9. **Involvement of Med-Arbiter in Litigation:**

   a) We agree not to request, subpoena, or demand the production of any record, notes, work product, or the like of the Med-Arbiter concerning his/her work with us. To the extent that we may have a right to demand these documents, that right is hereby waived.

   b) We agree that the Med-Arbiter shall not be called as a witness in any subsequent proceeding unless required by statute or court order.

10. **Witnesses:** We may stipulate to the Med-Arbiter consulting with expert witnesses and collaterals, such as therapists, custody evaluators, etc., outside of the mediation-arbitration session and agree that such information received may be considered by the Med-Arbiter in entering an award.

11. **Fees:**

    a) We agree to pay the Med-Arbiter for all time and costs of the mediation-arbitration, including time spent by the Med-Arbiter reviewing documents prior to mediation-arbitration; participating in mediation-arbitration sessions; phone conferences with attorneys, parties, and/or collaterals/experts; and deliberation and issuance of awards, at the rate of $ _____ per hour. We also agree to pay the costs of mediation-arbitration, including but not limited to long-distance telephone calls, copies, fax charges, etc.

b) We shall pay the mediation-arbitration fees and costs in the following manner: _____ shall pay _____ % and _____ shall pay _____ %. We understand that in the event we must reschedule or cancel an appointment, unless we notify the Med-Arbiter more than forty-eight (48) hours prior to the scheduled appointment, we will be billed for one hour of the Med-Arbiter's time. In the event that one of us does not appear for a scheduled appointment and has not given 48-hours advance notice and the other party does appear or is prepared to appear, the party who does not appear shall be responsible for both parties' fees. Nonpayment of fees shall be grounds for the resignation of the Med-Arbiter. We each shall deposit with the Med-Arbiter a retainer of $ _____ upon the signing of this Agreement. The Med-Arbiter shall only be entitled to any or all of the retainer as he/she spends time on our case. We will replenish the retainer to the level of $ _____ per party upon its depletion.

12. **Award:** Upon completion of the med-arb session, the Med-Arbiter shall issue an award in writing and deliver a copy of said award to each of us and to his/her respective attorney by U.S. mail, postage prepaid, within fourteen (14) days, or at a later date as circumstances may control, from the date of the completion of the session or receipt of the last written response from a party. The Med-Arbiter's final award shall be binding upon both parties pursuant to C.R.S. 14-10-128.5 _____(or other state statute)_____ and shall be filed by the Med-Arbiter with the District Court to be confirmed by the District Court in accordance with Section 13-22-213 C.R.S. _____(or other state statute)_____.

13. **Correction:** In most cases, the Med-Arbiter shall provide the parties with a draft award prior to filing the award with the Court. Any request for correction or modification of an award by the Med-Arbiter pursuant to Section 13-22-215 C.R.S. _____(or other state statute)_____ shall be directed to the Med

Arbiter first rather than to the District Court within seven (7) days of the award.

14. **Interviewing Children:** The Med-Arbiter is authorized to interview our child(ren) privately in order to ascertain the child's needs as to the issues being arbitrated. In conducting such an interview, the Med-Arbiter shall avoid forcing the child(ren) to choose between us.

15. **Time:** The Med-Arbiter is authorized to tell either or both of us if he/she believes that an inordinate amount of time is being taken by either or both of us. We agree that the amount of time spent on resolving the dispute be in proportion to the nature of the dispute, as determined by the Med-Arbiter.

16. **Term:** The term of the Med-Arbiter's service shall be a period of _____ months from the date of execution of this Agreement (from the later date if signed by us on different dates). At the end of the term, if one of us and/or the Med-Arbiter desire to terminate the professional relationship with the Med-Arbiter, this agreement shall be terminated. The service of the Med-Arbiter may be terminated prior to the end of the term if we both agree that we wish to terminate the Med-Arbiter's service or if the Med-Arbiter requests to withdraw prior to the termination date.

17. **Other Agreements:**

_____

Client

_____

Client

_____

Med-Arbiter

Signed this _____ day of _____ , _____ .

13

Special Master Agreement

The Special Master is the most commonly used model of neutral, third-party decision maker. A Special Master can be a fact finder, case manager, or med-arbiter. In addition, recommendations can be made to the court.

As a case manager, a Special Master may have an ongoing relationship with the high-conflict family with many of the same functions as a Parent Coordinator.

FORM 13–1:
SPECIAL MASTER AGREEMENT

SUPERIOR COURT OF CALIFORNIA, COUNTY OF SANTA CLARA

In re Marriage of:	)	Case No.
	)	
Petitioner:	)	STIPULATION AND
	)	ORDER APPOINTING
and	)	SPECIAL MASTER
	)	
Respondent:	)	
_____) APJ:		

Pursuant to the stipulation of the parties hereinafter set forth, and good cause appearing therefore, IT IS ORDERED, ADJUDGED, AND DECREED THAT:

A.   APPOINTMENT AND AUTHORITY

1.   _____ Tel: (   ) _____ is appointed Special Master under *Code of Civil Procedure* §638 until resignation, written agreement of the parties, further Court Order, or _____ (optional ending date), whichever first occurs. This appointment is based upon the expertise of the Special Master.

2.   Special Master shall have authority as set forth below to make decisions regarding the best interest of the child(ren), with the exception that the Special Master shall not have authority to make any order which changes legal or physical custody.

The Special Master may make the following types of orders in accordance with applicable constitutional and case law:

a) Ordering and changing: time share, visitation schedule or conditions (other than supervision), telephone, or correspondence contact;

b) Making and changing orders regarding exchange and/or transportation of the child(ren) including specifying time and place of exchange;

c) Ordering and changing education, day care, and/or extracurricular activities for the child(ren);

d) Making and changing orders regarding the alteration of the child(ren)'s appearance, such as haircuts, pierced ears, body piercing, tattoos;

e) Ordering either or both parents to substance-abuse testing and having access to any generated reports or results;

f) Making orders more specific so as to avoid violation of Court's orders.

3. In addition to the powers listed above in Paragraph 2, the Special Master may make the following orders in accordance with applicable constitutional and case law (check all applicable boxes):

❑ a. Changing the times for religious observances and training by the child(ren);

❑ b. Determining and ordering appropriate medical, mental health, and counseling treatment (including psychotherapy, substance abuse, and domestic violence counseling, and batterer's intervention prograrms, substance-abuse treatment or counseling, and parenting classes) for the child(ren) and the parents; the Special Master shall designate whether any ordered counseling is or is not confidential;

❑ c. Ordering psychological testing for either or both parents or the child(ren);

❑   d. Other:_____

   _____

   _____

   _____

   _____.

4. The Special Master may order the parties to an Emergency Screening at Family Court Services. The Order to Emergency Screening shall set forth a brief description of the nature of the emergency.

5. In an emergency, the Special Master may assist a party in obtaining an Emergency Protective Order through law enforcement and the Court.

6. The Special Master may request instructions from the Court, either in open court or in a writing directed to the court, with fifteen (15) days written notice to all parties, unless shortened by the Court. The parties may choose to respond.

7. On notice to both parties and the Court, the Special Master may recommend in writing or in open court that a custody evaluation or assessment be conducted. Such recommendation shall set forth the issues to be evaluated or assessed. Unless the parties agree to the evaluation or assessment within fifteen (15) days, the matter shall be set for a Case-Management Conference, at which the parties shall be present.

8. The Special Master may, on notice to both parties, recommend to the Court that an attorney be appointed for the minor child(ren). Such recommendation shall set forth the necessity for the appointment. If either party objects in writing to the recommendation within two (2) court days of the date the recommendation is made, the matter shall be set for a Case-Management Conference, at which the parties shall be present.

Objections shall be delivered to the clerk's office with a courtesy copy to the All-Purpose Judge's chambers.

9. The Special Master may make recommendations to the Court on the following additional issues: _____

_____

_____

B. QUASI-JUDICIAL IMMUNITY

1. The Special Master is an Officer of the Court, acting as a private judge for the parties to this action, to the extent of this Stipulation. The Special Master has quasi-judicial immunity. The Special Master cannot be sued based on his/her actions in this matter. The Special Master cannot be compelled to testify and is subject to the restrictions of Evidence Code §703.5.

2. The Special Master may not testify without the express agreement of the Special Master and the parties.

3. Notwithstanding the above, the Special Master may elect to testify in any hearing to remove the Special Master, in any request of the Special Master to the Court to terminate the appointment, in any request for instructions, or to enforce fee collection.

C. PROCEDURE

1. **Statement of Policies and Procedures:** The Special Master shall provide the parties with a written agreement for services containing his/her policies, including specifically the policy concerning confidentiality of information obtained by the Special Master, and the procedures used by the Special Master for dispute resolution. In the event the Special Master's policy is to receive and maintain confidential information, either party may

later request removal of the Special Master on this basis, to be considered by the Court in a good-cause request.

2. **Process:** Both parties shall participate in the dispute-resolution processes defined by the Special Master in accordance with principles of due process, which shall include at a minimum the opportunity for each of the parties to be heard. Each of the parties shall be present when so requested by the Special Master. In the event a party does not attend a meeting set by the Special Master, the Special Master may make orders despite the party's absence.

3. **Hearings:** The Special Master may conduct hearings either with the parties appearing personally or by telephone. Conference calls are encouraged. If either party wants an issue decided by the Special Master, he/she may submit a written or telephonic request to the Special Master, as directed by the Special Master, clearly setting forth the issues in dispute. The hearings may be informal and need not comply with the rules of hearsay or civil procedure. The testimony need not be sworn. **There is no confidentiality as to any evidence presented at such hearings.** If either party desires a record of the proceedings, on notice to the Special Master and the other party, he/she may, as may the Special Master, audiotape the proceedings or he/she may pay for a certified court reporter. Absent an emergency, the Special Master shall give the parties ten (10) days notice of such hearings. Either party may request an alternative date or time, which will be granted or denied based upon good cause shown.

4. **Interviews:** The Special Master may talk with and base orders or recommendations upon conversations with parties, attorneys, witnesses, or examinations of writings which take place without anyone by the Special Master. No record need be made. The Special Master may talk with each party and without the presence of either counsel. The Special Master shall have the authority to determine the protocol of all interviews, including the power to determine who attends such meetings.

5. **Decisions:** The Special Master must decide issues submitted within thirty (30) days from the submission of all applicable evidence. In the event that such a decision is not made within this time, the Court retains jurisdiction to resolve the dispute on noticed motion by either party.

6. **Child Abuse:** Notwithstanding any written policy of the Special Master, there is no confidentiality concerning communications with the Special Master regarding child abuse. **Incidents of child abuse or suspected child abuse that meet the mandatory reporting standards for mental health professionals will be reported by the Special Master to appropriate authorities.**

7. **Use of Assistants/Consultants:** On reasonable notice to the parties, the Special Master may utilize consultants and/or assistants as necessary to aid the Special Master in the performance of the duties contained herein. Fees for such consultants or assistants will be advanced by the parties as directed by the Special Master. In making such directions, the Special Master will consider the financial circumstances of the parties. In the event of a dispute regarding the allocation of such fees, the Court retains jurisdiction to resolve the dispute.

D. DECISIONS

Decisions of the Special Master shall be subject to the following forms of judicial review:

1. Orders made by the Special Master, if in writing, shall be binding and effective when signed by the Special Master. Orders need not be in writing and may be made orally, if circumstances involving severe time constraints and/or possible emergencies so warrant. Oral orders shall be binding and effective when made in a fashion communicated to both parties, and such orders shall be further confirmed in writing to both parties and counsel as soon as practicable. Orders will be submitted to a

Judge at a later time, but their date of effectiveness is as stated in this paragraph.

2. The Special Master will issue a written Statement of Decision, setting forth the reasons for an order or recommendation, if requested by either party within five (5) days of the issuance of the order or recommendation. The Special Master may issue a Statement of Decision with any order or recommendation.

3. **An order to show cause or motion challenging an order that is effective as set forth in Paragraph (D)(1), above, must be filed no later than fifteen (15) calendar days after the date of mailing the Special Master's order. Failure to do so without just cause shall be dispositive of the issue.** Notwithstanding any other provisions of the local Court Rules to the contrary, the filing of the motion is all that is legally required to constitute a challenge to the entirety of the Special Master's order; the motion shall include a detailed statement of the specific objections to the Special Master's order. The order of the Special Master shall remain effective unless specifically set aside or modified by an order of the Court.

Prior to the scheduled hearing, the parties and counsel, if requested by the parties, shall meet and confer with the Special Master to attempt to resolve the objections. In the event that the issues are resolved, a written stipulation shall be prepared by the Special Master or counsel and submitted to the Court prior to the hearing. The Special Master's orders or decision may be vacated or corrected on any of the applicable grounds specified in *CCP*§§641.1286.2 and 1286.6.

4. Any party challenging an order or recommendation of the Special Master shall have the burden of proving that the recommendation or order should not be adopted.

5. **Copies of all motions, objections, or other documents submitted to the Court or issued by the Court shall be served in accordance with *CCP*§§1005 on all parties, counsel, and the Special Master by the person or entity generating such documents.**

E. COMMUNICATION WITH SPECIAL MASTER

1. The parties and their attorneys shall have the right to initiate or receive ex-parte communication with the Special Master. Provided, however, ex-parte communications should be minimized whenever possible and the Special Master shall have the right to disclose all ex-parte communications. If the Special Master is requested to make orders based upon an ex-parte communication, he/she shall make reasonable efforts to contact the other party before making such orders and, if required, to schedule a hearing in accordance with Paragraph 3 above. A party or witness who initiates contact in writing with the Special Master must provide copies to all parties simultaneously.

2. The Special Master may not communicate ex-parte with the Judge, provided, however, that the Special Master may communicate in writing to the Judge, so long as copies are sent to the parties and their counsel.

3. Counsel for ❑ Petitioner/Plaintiff ❑ Respondent/Defendant shall provide, within fifteen (15) calendar days of the date this order is mailed, copies of all:

   ❑ Pleadings

   ❑ Orders and correspondence between counsel or the Court and counsel related to the action

F. DATA COLLECTION

The parties have been informed that they are not required to give up privileges or rights to privacy, and they do not have to agree to disclose information. However, they agree that records and information regarding either party and/or the child(ren) may be released to the Special Master by the following:

1. Child(ren)'s current/previous pediatrician

2. Child(ren)'s current/previous psychologist/psychiatrist or mental health professional

3. Child(ren)'s current/previous teacher(s) and schools

4. Hospital and medical records of child(ren)'s current/previous physician

5. Law-enforcement agencies, police department/sheriff's office

6. Prior Special Master

7. Custody Evaluator

8. Day-care providers

9. Other: _____.

The parties will sign the consent to release of the above-listed information form(s) provided to them by the Special Master. In addition, the parties shall provide nonprivileged documents to the Special Master on request.

G.   FEES

1. **Charges and Costs:** The Special Master's hourly fee shall be set by the Special Master pursuant to an agreement between the parties and the Special Master. Said fees shall not exceed $ _____ per hour. It is understood that despite the fact that the Special Master may make decisions or orders in favor of one party, both parties will continue to be responsible for the payment of fees associated with such services at the allocated percentage designated in Section H below. Ultimately, the Court shall determine the proper allocation between the parties of the fees of the Special Master for such services and may require reimbursement by one party to the other for any payment to the Special Master.

The Special Master shall be reimbursed for any reasonable expense he/she incurs in association with his/her role as Special Master. These costs may include, but are not limited to, the following: photocopies, messenger service, long-distance telephone charges, express and/or certified mail costs and excess postage to foreign countries, parking, tolls, mileage and travel expenses, and word processing at a rate of $ _____ per hour.

In the event that either party fails to provide twenty-four-hours' (24-hours') notice of cancellation of any appointment with the Special Master, such party shall pay all of the Special Master's charges of such missed appointment at the full hourly rate, at the discretion of the Special Master.

Telephone calls to the Special Master by either party are part of the process and appropriately paid for by the parties according to their percentage share as ordered, unless otherwise determined by the Special Master.

2. **Payments:** Prior to the initial interview, the parties will provide the Special Master with an advance retainer totaling $ _____ , $ _____ from each party. The aforementioned hourly fees and costs as set forth above shall be drawn against this retainer. Any funds remaining at the termination of the Special Master's services shall be refunded to the parties. In the event the retainer is expended prior to the termination of the Special Master's services, the parties agree to provide a like amount as and for an additional advance retainer within fifteen (15) days of the request. The Special Master shall not become a creditor of the parties.

3. **Objections to Fees or Costs:** Any objection to the Special Master's bills must be brought to his/her attention in written form within thirty (30) business days of the billing date, otherwise the billing shall be deemed accepted.

4. **Enforcement:** In the event that a legal action becomes necessary to enforce any provision of this order, the nonprevailing party

shall pay actual and reasonable attorney's fees and costs as may
be incurred. The Special Master may proceed by noticed motion
to the Court in the event his/her fees are not timely paid. A
willful failure to advance an initial or later retainer within fifteen
(15) days of a demand therefore may be the subject of monetary
or issue sanctions or a contempt action.

H.   ALLOCATIONS

Except as otherwise provided herein, the fees of the Special Master
shall be shared by the parties in the following manner:

Father shall pay _____ % of the Special Master's fees, expenses,
and advance deposit; and

Mother shall pay _____ % of the Special Master's fees, expenses,
and advance deposit.

The Special Master shall have the right to *recommend* the re-
allocation of payment of his/her fees at a percentage different from the
above if he/she believes the need for his/her services is attributable to
the conduct of one party or if changed financial circumstances of one
party or both parties warrant it.

I.   RENEWAL, WITHDRAWAL, REMOVAL, GRIEVANCES

1. **Renewal of Term of Appointment:** The parties and the Special
   Master may agree to renew or extend the term of the Special
   Master by written stipulation and order.

2. **Withdrawal of the Special Master:** The Special Master may, on
   notice to all parties and counsel, ask that the Court remove
   him/her as Special Master. Such request shall set forth the
   reason for such request.

3. **Removal of the Special Master:** The Special Master can be
   removed or replaced at any time by written stipulation and order
   signed by all parties. In the event the parties do not agree to

remove the Special Master, either party may request the removal of the Special Master by noticed motion on any of the grounds applicable to the removal of a Judge, Referee, or Arbitrator, or on showing of good cause in the event it is the written policy of the Special Master to receive or maintain confidential information. Such motion shall proceed on the written documents submitted by both parties and the Special Master, unless the Court orders an evidentiary hearing. Each party and the Special Master may respond to the initial submissions in writing.

4. **Grievances:** Any complaints or grievances from either party regarding the performance or actions of the Special Master shall be dealt with according to the following procedure:

a) A person having a complaint or grievance regarding the Special Master must discuss the matter with the Special Master in person before pursuing it in any other manner.

b) If, after discussion, the party decides to pursue a complaint, he/she must then submit a written letter detailing the complaint or grievance to the Special Master, to the other party, to both parties' attorneys (if any), and to the attorney for the child(ren), if one exists. The Special Master will within thirty (30) days provide a written response to the grievance to both parties, both attorneys, and the attorney for the child(ren).

c) If appropriate, given the circumstances, the Special Master will then meet with the parties and their attorneys (if any) to discuss the matter.

d) If the grievance or complaint is not resolved after this meeting, the complaining party may proceed by noticed motion to the Court for removal of Special Master as specified above.

e) The Court shall reserve jurisdiction to determine if either or both parties' and/or the Special Master shall ultimately be responsible for any portions or all of said Special Master's time and costs spent in responding to the grievance and the Special Master's attorney's fees, if any.

J. WAIVER OF RULE OF COURT 244.1

Both parties agree that the Special Master shall be advised of the grounds for objection to appointment under *CCP*§641, and the Special Master shall disclose to both parties or their counsel if represented within thirty (30) days the existence of any such grounds. The failure of either party to file with the Court within fifteen (15) days any objection under *CCP*§641 shall be deemed a waiver of grounds for objection to the Special Master under *CCP*§641. Both parties agree that the requirement to post a notice indicating the case number and telephone number of the person to contact to arrange for attendance in any Special Master proceeding under *California Rule of Court* 244.1(C) is waived. To that extent, the records in this case are deemed confidential.

K. DELIVERY TO FAMILY COURT SERVICES

The Petitioner/Plaintiff shall forthwith deliver a copy of this stipulation and order to Family Court Services.

L. CONSENT

The parties acknowledge and initial the following.

____ / ____   I understand that a Special Master can only be appointed with my agreement and I agree to the appointment of the Special Master named in this stipulation.

____ / ____   I understand that I can limit the issues before the Special Master. I have reviewed the issues that are to be decided by the Special Master in this stipulation and I agree to each of them.

____ / ____   I understand that I can limit the time that the Special Master serves and that the powers of the Special Master will end at the end of the appointment term. I agree to the term of the appointment of the Special Master in this stipulation.

___ / ___ I understand that the orders of the Special Master can be reviewed by the Court but that an objection must be made within the time specified in this stipulation.

___ / ___ I have had an opportunity to confer with the Special Master appointed in this stipulation, I have received this Special Master's written statement of policies and procedures, and I agree to this Special Master's appointment.

___ / ___ I understand that the Special Master cannot be called as a witness if I object to the Special Master's order.

___ / ___ I have had an opportunity to review this stipulation and to have questions about this stipulation answered by legal counsel.

AGREED:

Dated: _____   Dated: _____

_____   _____
Father   Mother

_____   _____
Attorney for Father   Attorney for Mother

I agree to my appointment as Special Master contained in this stipulation.

Dated: _____   _____
                                  Special Master

ORDER

IT IS SO ORDERED:

Dated: _____   _____
                                          Judicial Officer

14

Court-Ordered Parenting Coordination

Massachusetts judges can appoint Parenting Coordinators using their equity powers. A PC can create a parenting plan or monitor compliance with one that is already in place.

The legislature in Vermont, through the Vermont Court Administrator's Office, has made funds available to subsidize parenting coordination on a sliding-fee basis. Parent coordination is initiated by an "order of referral for parent coordination" and is provided by contract mediators. Protocols have been developed that are complied with by these specially trained contract mediators. Forms 14–1 through 14–4 cover these areas.

FORM 14–1:
PARENTING-COORDINATOR AGREEMENT

1. We, _____ and _____
   have been ordered by the Hon. _____ of
   the Probate and Family Court held in _____
   to engage the services of _____ who will
   serve as Parenting Coordinator (PC) for us and our children.

2. The Court has ordered that the services of the PC shall be paid
   as follows: father's share _____ %, mother's share _____ %.
   The PC reserves the right to alter this payment arrangement if,
   in the judgment of the PC, one parent or the other creates
   unnecessary problems in the resolution of an issue, unnecessarily generates conflict, or in other ways utilizes a dispropor-
   tionate amount of the PC's time.

   a. Retainers for service shall be paid by each parent in
   accordance with the percentages detailed above. Both parties
   shall receive thorough accountings for all time, activities, and
   costs associated with these services. The cost of services shall
   be deducted from the retainer. Once the retainer falls below
   $ _____ , it will be brought up to $ _____ , proportionately by
   each party within ten (10) days or services may be suspended.
   At the end of the parent-coordination process, any remaining
   retainer shall be distributed according to the proportions
   above within thirty (30) days.

   b. The PC reserves the right to file with the Court a
   Motion or Complaint to collect payment. The party(s) shall be
   responsible for all costs and time associated with these actions.

3. The services of the PC are at a rate of $ _____ per hour. This
   cost of the services includes, but is not limited to, time
   expended for interviews, record reviews, telephone calls, document preparation, court testimony, and travel time.

4. The PC's work with the family is not confidential, in that either
   party may subpoena the PC to testify in court. In this case, the

party who issues the subpoena shall be responsible for the costs of the record review and court time, including travel, parking, and other incidental costs.

5. The parent-coordination process is a form of alternative dispute resolution, which includes assisted negotiations and arbitration. Every effort shall be made by the parties to resolve differences themselves in a mutually satisfactory manner. If issues are not resolved, then the PC shall engage in mediation between the parties to resolve disputes. If efforts to mediate resolution of an issue(s) are unsuccessful, then the PC shall resolve the issue through arbitration. The decisions of the PC will apply until such time that either party brings the case back to the Probate and Family Court and the Court rules on the matter. The overriding concern in the resolution of all issues is the best interest of the child(ren).

6. All agreements between the parties shall be forwarded to the PC Coordinator.

7. The Parenting Coordinator shall share all correspondence with both parties except those, if any, required for submission to the Court. Copies of those documents may be obtained by the parties' attorneys.

8. Appointments or telephone contacts with the PC may be scheduled at the request of either parent or of the PC. All parties agree to make a good-faith effort to be available when contacts are requested.

9. This agreement cannot cover all the particulars that may arise in every situation. The parties agree that the PC may need to establish new rules and guidelines to fit their unique relationship.

10. If the PC deems himself/herself no longer able to work with either party in an unbiased manner then he/she may notify the

Court of that situation and request that the appointment be vacated. In that event the PC may suggest to the parties the names of other potential PCs.

11. If either party wishes to terminate the services of the PC and the other party does not agree, an order of the Court is required to remove him/her.

12. We are aware that the PC, as a licensed mental health professional, is required by law to report any suspected physical or sexual abuse of the child(ren) to the appropriate authorities. We are also aware that the PC has a duty to warn if believable threats are made by one or the other party or if either party poses a potential threat to himself/herself.

I have read the above agreement and have had the opportunity to discuss it with my attorney if I so wished. I enter into this agreement with the full understanding that if I cannot resolve conflicts with my ex-spouse, the PC will have the right to make decisions that will affect me and my child(ren). The parties always retain the right to bring the case back to the Court for review.

I understand and agree to all of the above.

_____	_____
Client	Date
_____	_____
Client	Date
_____	_____
Parenting Coordinator	Date

_____

Used with permission of Linda Cavallero, Ph.D., and Joseph McGill, LCSW.

FORM 14–2:
ORDER OF REFERRAL FOR PARENTING COORDINATION

STATE OF _____   _____ FAMILY COURT

_____ COUNTY, SS.   DOCKET NO. _____

_____

VS.

_____

The above entitled matter came before the _____ Family
Court on ___(date)___ . Based upon the agreement of the parties, it is
hereby ORDERED:

1. The Court hereby appoints _____ to serve
   as Parent Coordinator (PC) in the above entitled matter for the
   purpose of resolving issues related to parent–child contact.

2. The PC shall assist the parties in developing a parenting plan for
   the children in accordance with the attached protocol. Specifically, the PC shall:

   a) Meet with each party, separately or together at his/her
   discretion. In addition, the PC may meet with any child(ren);
   persons who have relationships with the child(ren); and professionals who have provided services to the child(ren) or the
   parents.

   b) Make recommendations to the parties regarding parent–
   child contact schedules, safety issues, drop-off and pick-up arrangements, and other child-related concerns consistent with the best
   interests of the children. The PC may also refer the parties to
   services in the community that are necessary to the implementation of the parenting plan and the creation of a safe environment for the child(ren). The recommendations of the PC shall
   be in writing with copies to the Court.

c) If the parties reach agreement regarding a parenting plan, the PC's recommendations shall be accompanied by a signed memoranda of agreement between the parents.

d) If the parties are unable to reach agreement regarding a parenting plan, the PC shall file a recommended parenting plan with the Court. The PC's recommendations may also address the need to have certain issues heard by the Court in a contested hearing and/or the need for a home study or forensic evaluation.

e) If either party objects to the parenting plan recommended by the PC, he/she shall file written objections within ten (10) days following the filing of the PC's recommended plan. After reviewing the recommendations and the objections, the Court will schedule the matter for hearing to discuss the objections and determine whether to adopt the PC's recommendations in whole or in part.

f) Pending a court hearing, the PC is authorized to direct the parties to follow an interim parent–child contact schedule if he/she believes that this is in the best interests of the child(ren).

3. The parties shall participate in parent coordination in accordance with the attached protocols.

4. Each parent shall be responsible for contacting the PC to set up an initial interview. _____ (Parent Coordinator) may be reached at _____ (telephone number).

5. Each parent shall be responsible for signing releases to permit the PC to contact professionals who have provided services to the child(ren) or themselves.

Dated _____   _____ (city/state)

_____
Presiding Judge

Release of Information

I hereby grant _____ , an agent of the _____ (state) Family Court Parent-Coordination Program (or relevant program), permission to discuss with any person, professional, or agency whose opinions and information may be relevant to my child(ren)'s well-being. These matters may involve the Custody, Parental Rights and Responsibilities, and/or Parent–Child Contact arrangements involving my child(ren).

_____   _____
Child's Name   Date of Birth

_____   _____
Child's Name   Date of Birth

_____   _____
Child's Name   Date of Birth

_____   _____
Child's Name   Date of Birth

_____
Parent's Name

_____   _____
Parent's Signature   Date

_____

Used with permission of Jennifer Barker, Vermont Family Court Mediation Program, Parent Coordination Services.

FORM 14–3:
VERMONT FAMILY COURT MEDIATION PROGRAM
PARENTING-COORDINATION PROTOCOLS

Definition of Parenting Coordination

An alternative dispute-resolution process for parents for whom mediation is inappropriate due to high level of conflict or domestic abuse in the relationship. The service is offered to separated parents to assist in developing safe, workable plans on behalf of their child(ren).

Definition of Domestic Abuse

Either physical, psychological, or verbal actions which are intended to, and have the effect of, control, coercion, intimidation, physical harm, or cause fear on the part of a family member (see VFCMP Domestic Abuse Protocols, 12/94 version).

Program Protocols

Under the terms of the Vermont Family Court Mediation Program, all contract mediators agree to abide by the Domestic Abuse Protocols established in December 1994 (see attached).

Mediators whose contract with the Court Administrator has been amended to permit offering parenting coordination to parents who would otherwise be ineligible for mediation services shall abide by the following:

1. Participation in parenting coordination may be requested by either parent, by the Family Court judge, or by the parties' attorneys. In most cases, participation is a voluntary effort by the parents to resolve child-related issues in a nonadversarial process. In cases where parenting coordination is ordered by the judge, impasses may be resolved by the Parent Coordinator (PC).

    1.1 Initial parenting-coordination conferences are scheduled separately. Whether subsequent conferences will be held jointly or individually will be at the discretion of the PC. Whether a situation requires a conference at the courthouse (or other location) or by telephone will also be at the discretion of the PC.

1.2 If the PC detects the use of alcohol or other drug-related impairment during a conference, that conference will be canceled.

1.3 In addition to developing parenting plans, the PC may make referrals to services in the community that are necessary to implementing plans and creating a safe, nonviolent environment for children.

1.4 The PC may attend hearings on parental rights and responsibilities and relief from abuse hearings.

1.5 All stipulations must be reviewed, approved, and signed by the Judge before being incorporated into a court order.

1.6 Motions for modification or enforcement must be filed by the parents or their attorneys—not the PC.

2. Parenting coordination is a nonconfidential, child-centered process.

2.1 The goal of parenting coordination is to develop plans that reduce the risk of children's exposure to parental conflict.

2.2 Parents will sign a release of information form that allows the PC to consult with a court-appointed Guardian *ad litem* or professionals in the community involved with the child(ren).

2.3 The PC may make recommendations about visitation schedules, safety issues, drop-off and pick-up arrangements, and other child-related concerns.

2.4 The PC may meet one or more times with the child(ren) in their home or in a community setting to allow them the opportunity to express their thoughts directly to the PC.

2.5   Recommendations and referrals made to the parents by the PC will be in writing, with copies to attorneys and the court file.

2.6   Signed memoranda of agreement between the parents will be placed in the court file.

2.7   If the PC discovers that a child is being inappropriately touched or otherwise abused, a report will be made to the Dept. of SRS. Likewise, if threats of violence are directed at one parent by the other, those threats will be reported to both the police and the court.

3. The PC reserves the right to terminate the dispute resolution process if either parent or the child(ren) are being endangered by the process.

Used with permission of Jennifer Barker, Vermont Family Court Mediation Program, Parent Coordination Services.

FORM 14–4:
STIPULATION REGARDING
PARENT COORDINATION

STATE OF VERMONT   VERMONT FAMILY COURT

ADDISON COUNTY, SS.   DOCKET NO.

(plaintiff)

        VS.

(defendant)

Based upon the agreement of the parties. It is hereby STIPULATED that:

1. _____ shall serve as Parenting Coordinator (PC) in the above entitled matter for the purpose of resolving issues related to parent–child contact.

2. The PC shall assist the parties in developing a parenting plan for the child(ren) in accordance with the attached protocol. Specifically, the PC shall:

    a) Meet with each parent separately. In addition, the PC may meet with child(ren); persons who have relationships with the child(ren); and professionals who have provided services to the child(ren) or the parents.

    b) Make recommendations to the parties regarding parent–child contact schedules, safety issues, drop-off and pick-up arrangements and other child-related concerns consistent with the best interests of the child(ren). The PC may also refer the parties to services in the community that are necessary to the implementation of the parenting plan and the creation of a safe environment for the child(ren). The recommendations of the PC shall be in writing to the parents and attorneys of record, with copies to the Court.

c) If the parties reach agreement regarding a parenting plan, the PC's recommendations shall be accompanied by a signed memoranda of agreement between the parents.

d) If the parties are unable to reach agreement regarding a parenting plan, the PC shall file a recommended parenting plan with the Court. The PC's recommendations may also address the need to have certain issues heard by the Court in a contested hearing and/or the need for a home study or forensic evaluation.

e) If either party objects to the parenting plan recommended by the PC, he/she shall file written objections within ten (10) days following the filing of the PC's recommended plan. After reviewing the recommendations and the objections, the Court will schedule the matter for hearing to discuss the objections and determine whether to adopt the PC's recommendations in whole or in part.

f) Pending a court hearing, the PC is authorized to direct the parties to follow an interim parent–child contact schedule if he/she believes that this is in the best interests of the child(ren).

3. The parties shall participate in parenting coordination in accordance with the attached protocols.

4. Each parent shall be responsible for contacting the PC.

5. Each parent shall be responsible for signing releases to permit the PC to contact professionals who have provided services to the child(ren) or themselves.

6. Parent coordination is available with the following conditions:

a) Subsidized services are offered up to twenty (20) hours per family, including office conferences, telephone conferences, courthouse hearings, meetings with the child(ren), and consultation with professionals who have provided family services. The twenty-hour limit per family also includes writing of agreements and recommendations.

b) Each parent shall be responsible for his/her co-payment for up to ten (10) hours of parenting coordination according to the financial agreement.

Signed _____ Date _____

Signed _____ Date _____

Used with permission of Jennifer Barker, Vermont Family Court Mediation Program, Parent Coordination Services.

15

Appointment of a Special Advocate

In Colorado, the court, by a motion of either party, may appoint a special advocate to resolve issues related to the children or to high-conflict issues between the parents. The special advocate can investigate, report, and make recommendations. The duties must be clearly specified in the order of appointment.

Form 15–1 is a Motion for Appointment of a Special Advocate.

Form 15–2 is an Order Appointing a Special Advocate.

Forms 15–3 and 15–4 each contain a sample Special Advocate contract.

FORM 15–1:
MOTION FOR APPOINTMENT
OF A SPECIAL ADVOCATE

DISTRICT COURT, _____ COUNTY, COLORADO

Case No. _____   Div./Ctrm. _____

_____

_____

In re the Marriage of:

* * Petitioner,

                              and

* * Respondent.

_____

The Special Advocate is needed because this case involves:

( ) an unborn child   ( ) high conflict between the
                                     parents

( ) determination of   ( ) allegations of abuse
    paternity

( ) a special-needs child   ( ) other _____

_____

_____

The Special Advocate is needed to investigate and make recommendations to the Court concerning:

( ) custody   ( ) property division

( ) parenting time   ( ) allegations of abuse

( ) conflicts between the   ( ) potential dependency/
    parties   neglect issues

( ) other _____

_____

_____

Recommendations as to Special Advocate:

1. Name _____

   Address _____

   _____

   Telephone _____

2. Qualifications _____

   _____

3. Cost $ _____

   Retainer $ _____

The fees of the Special Advocate shall initially be paid by:

_____

_____

   ❑ Petitioner   ❑ Respondent

FORM 15–2:
ORDER APPOINTING SPECIAL ADVOCATE

DISTRICT COURT, * * COUNTY, COLORADO

Case No. _____   Div./Ctrm. _____

_____

_____

In re the Marriage of:

* * Petitioner,

                              and

* * Respondent.

_____

The Court, having reviewed _____ Motion for Appointment of a Special Advocate, and the Court file, thus finds that the appointment of a Special Advocate is necessary to protect the best interests of the minor child(ren), pursuant to C.R.S. §14-10-116(2)(b) and C.R.S. §14-10-124.

It is therefore ordered that * *, whose address and telephone number is * *, is appointed the child(ren)'s Special Advocate to investigate, report, and make recommendations in the best interests of the child(ren). The Special Advocate shall comply with the requirements of Chief Justice Directive 97-02.

The parties shall arrange to have their first meeting with the Special Advocate within _____ days of the effective date of this order and shall confer with the Special Advocate as directed by the Special Advocate. Parties and their counsel shall cooperate with the Special Advocate in his/her investigation. The Special Advocate may consider a party's cooperation or lack of cooperation as a factor in making his/her recommendations.

Counsel for Petitioner/Respondent shall promptly provide the Special Advocate with complete and legible copies of all pleadings and documents herein.

For this case, the subject matter and scope of the Special Advocate's responsibilities shall be as follows:

Rule 35 Evaluation. The Special Advocate shall perform an evaluation of the mental condition of the _____ .
The time, place, manner, and conditions and scope of the evaluation
shall be as follows: _____

_____

_____

_____

_____

Evaluation of Parenting

_____ Evaluation of the parenting history and the quality of the
parenting

_____ Observations and evaluation of parent–child interactions

_____ Evaluation of the current living arrangements and current
parenting-time patterns

Evaluation of Child(ren)

_____ Evaluation of the special needs of the child(ren) including:

    _____ Learning disabilities

    _____ Intellectual disabilities

    _____ Medical needs

    _____ Attachment issues

    _____ Emotional needs

    _____ Behavioral assessment

    _____ Child(ren)'s adjustment to the divorce

_____ Evaluation of child abuse—physical and/or sexual abuse and/
or neglect

Evaluation of Parent Communication

_____   Evaluation of the parents' dispute

_____   Evaluation of the parents' capacity to be joint custodians and special factors which might preclude joint custody

Evaluation of Domestic Abuse

_____   Domestic violence evaluation of _____

Evaluation of Substance Abuse

_____   Drug and/or alcohol abuse evaluation of _____

Other

_____

_____

_____

_____

In general, the subject matter and scope of the Special Advocate's responsibilities shall be as follows:

1. To meet personally with the child(ren) and to inform him/herself about those aspects of the parties, their child(ren), and the family relevant to the issues of appointment.

2. Upon presentation of a certified copy of this order to any agency, hospital, organization, school, person, or office, including the clerk of this court, pediatrician, psychologist, psychiatrist, law enforcement agency, or social service agency, the Special Advocate shall be permitted to inspect and copy records relevant to custody and parenting-time issues.

3. The Special Advocate may consult with any person who may have information relevant to the issues of appointment and obtain information from medical, mental health, educational, or other expert persons who have served the child(ren) in the past without obtaining the consent of the parent or the child(ren)'s custodian.

4. The Special Advocate shall maintain information received from any source as confidential, and it shall not be disclosed except in reports filed with the Court in this action, to the parties in this action, and their respective counsel, or as further authorized by order of the Court.

5. To attend all court hearings and to testify as a witness concerning his/her activities and recommendations, if and when requested to do so by either party or by the Court.

6. After the Special Advocate has thoroughly and independently investigated the issues affecting the minor child(ren), the Special Advocate shall file a clear, concise written report setting forth independent and informed recommendations to the Court regarding the best interests of the child(ren) at least _____ days prior to any hearing. The child(ren)'s wishes, if expressed, shall be included in this report and considered by the Special Advocate, but the Special Advocate need not adopt these wishes in his/her recommendations to the Court.

7. The Special Advocate shall bring to the attention of the court any ethical concerns that may arise during the performance of his/her duties as a Special Advocate.

The Special Advocate shall be immune from any civil or criminal liability to the maximum extent permitted by law, and shall continue to serve until further order of the Court.

If it is the opinion of the Special Advocate that the services of other professionals or an extended evaluation by the Special Advocate would be of benefit to the parties and/or their child(ren), or would assist the

Special Advocate in preparing the report and/or recommendations, the Special Advocate shall so advise the Court and counsel in writing. No such services of other professionals shall be provided unless agreed to by both parties or ordered by the Court.

Unless and until otherwise agreed by the parties or Court Order, the Special Advocate's fees and expenses shall be paid _____ % by the Petitioner and _____ % by Respondent, and shall be paid within thirty (30) days of the date billed. The Special Advocate's services shall be billed at an hourly rate of $ _____. The Petitioner shall pay $ _____ and the Respondent shall pay $ _____ as an initial retainer to the Special Advocate.

DONE AND SIGNED this ____ day of _____ , 20 ____.

_____

DISTRICT COURT JUDGE/MAGISTRATE

FORM 15–3:
SPECIAL ADVOCATE CONTRACT

We, _____ and _____ understand that _____(professional's name)_____ has been appointed by the Court as a Special Advocate for our child(ren), _____ _____. We have received a copy of the Court's Order Re: Special Advocate, dated _____ , have read it, and have discussed any questions we have regarding it with _____(professional's name)_____.

1. We understand that as a Special Advocate, _____(professional's name)'s_____ primary responsibility is to serve our child(ren)'s best interest. His/her goal is to help us resolve our differences regarding the child(ren) and their care in a manner that serves the child(ren)'s best interest, minimizes conflict between us that could harm the child(ren), and fosters cooperation between us as their parents.

2. We understand that _____(professional's name)_____ is a trained clinical social worker and has knowledge of child development, family dynamics, and psychological functioning. We understand that we will have the benefit of this knowledge in our work with him/her but that he/she is not functioning as a psychotherapist for either of us or our child(ren). He/She may help us understand our child(ren)'s developmental needs and the psychological dynamics operating in our family. He/She may also help us learn effective communication and problem-solving skills. Because of the provisions of the Special Advocate statute that the Special Advocate shall investigate, make recommendations, and report to the Court and may be called to testify, none of the information gathered by _____(professional's name)_____ can be regarded as confidential.

3. We understand that _____(professional's name)_____ is a trained mediator and may use his/her facilitation skills to help us communicate and collaborate more effectively. Because of the

provisions of the Special Advocate statute, the usual neutrality and confidentiality associated with the formal mediation process do not apply. ____(professional's name)____ will retain as his/her primary responsibility to serve the best interests of the child(ren) and he/she will issue recommendations with his/her report. Any agreements we have reached will be incorporated into his/her report as long as he/she believes they are in the child(ren)'s best interest.

4. We understand that _____(professional's name)_____ is not functioning as a custody evaluator as defined by Colorado law.

5. We agree to pay _____(professional's name)_____ $ _____ an hour for his/her time, including but not limited to that spent reviewing documents, interviewing the parties and the child(ren), drafting reports or recommendations, and in phone contact with the parties or phone conferences with attorneys and/or other professionals. We understand we shall also be billed for related expenses, including but not limited to long-distance telephone calls, copies, fax charges, etc. Any testimony (and associated travel and waiting time) is charged at the rate of $ _____ per hour. We will divide the fees as follows:

_____

_____.

We agree to pay an initial retainer of $ _____ prior to our first appointment. We will divide the retainer as follows: _____

_____.

We understand that we will be responsible for any charges over the initial retainer amount and that unless we have made other arrangements with ____(professional's name)____, balances not paid within thirty (30) days may be subject to interest of _____ % per month (_____ % annual). We understand that fees must be paid in full before ____(professional's name)____ will release his/her report or testify in Court. If the full retainer amount is not used, ____(professional's name)____ will return it to us in the same proportion it was paid by us.

6. We understand that in the event we must reschedule or cancel an appointment, unless we notify the Special Advocate twenty-four (24) hours prior to the scheduled appointment, we will be billed for one hour of the Special Advocate's time. If one of us does not appear for a scheduled joint session, has not given 24-hours' notice, and the other party does appear, the first party shall be responsible for both parties' portion of the fee.

7. We agree to make ourselves and our child(ren) available for appointments with _____(professional's name)_____ .

8. We authorize _____(professional's name)_____ to interview our child(ren) privately in order to ascertain what is in their best interest. In conducting such interviews, _____(professional's name)_____ will avoid forcing the child(ren) to choose between us or to reject either of us.

9. We understand that _____(professional's name)_____ may need to gather information from other individuals with knowledge of our family, such as school personnel, psychotherapists, day-care providers, or other family members. We agree to authorize other professionals or individuals to communicate with _____(professional's name)_____ upon his/her request.

10. We understand that _____(professional's name)_____ is required by law to report any physical or sexual abuse of the child(ren) to the appropriate authorities and that he/she also has a duty to warn if believable threats are made by one party to any other party or if he/she believes either party is a potential threat to him-/herself.

11. We understand that _____(professional's name)_____ may need to call us from his/her home phone (especially in the evening and on weekends) and that he/she may use call blocking. We understand that he/she may not be able to reach us if we employ call blocking.

I have read, understand, and agree to each of the provisions of this agreement.

I have read, understand, and agree to each of the provisions of this agreement.

_____

Signature   Date

_____

Signature   Date

_____

(Professional's Name) (Special Advocate)   Date

FORM 15–4:
SPECIAL ADVOCATE CONTRACT

We, _____ and _____
understand that ____(professional's name)____ has been appointed by
the Court as Special Advocate for our child(ren): _____

_____

A copy of the court order appointing a Special Advocate is attached to
this contract. We have read the contract and discussed any questions we
have regarding it with ____(professional's name)____ .

1. We understand that as a Special Advocate, ____(professional's
   name)'s____ primary responsibility is to serve our child(ren)'s
   best interests.

2. We understand that, as a Special Advocate, ____(professional's
   name)____ is responsible to the Court and may be required to
   file periodic reports to the Court as to the progress in and/or
   results of tasks defined in the court order.

3. We understand that ____(professional's name)____ must, by
   law, report any suspected sexual or physical abuse or neglect of
   a child. It is not his/her role to determine the validity of the
   suspected abuse, only that it is a possibility. Others have the
   duty to determine validity. In addition, ____(professional's
   name)____ has the duty to warn if believable threats are made
   by one party against another party, or if he/she believes that
   either party is a threat to him/herself (i.e., suicide).

4. We understand that ____(professional's name)____ is not an
   attorney and cannot offer legal advice. Each party should keep
   a consulting attorney to make sure of any legal implications in
   agreements reached.

5. We understand that ____(professional's name)____ is a licensed clinical psychologist with a specialty in children and

families. He/She has knowledge of child development, family dynamics, psychological functioning, and the impact of divorce on adults and children. He/She has conducted custody evaluations and parenting responsibility evaluations. In addition he/she has taken _____ courses in mediation. He/She also has experience as a parenting coordinator, a Special Advocate, a mediator, and a mediator-arbitrator.

6. _____(Professional's name)_____ is paid at the rate of $ _____ per hour. This is calculated, if necessary, in _____-minute increments, so _____ minutes would be billed as one (1) hour. Payment may be made in one of two formats. All parties must pay within the same format. Expert witness time is charged at $ _____ per hour and begins when ____(professional's name)____ reaches the courthouse. There will be a prearranged travel charge for more-distant counties. Deposition time is billed at $ _____ an hour. Preparation time for court or depositions is charged at the $ _____ rate.

FORMAT I: Payment is made at the close of each session. If payment is not available when this format is chosen, all Special Advocate activities will be suspended until payment is received. Report writing and other non-face-to-face time will be billed and paid at the next meeting. The Court will be informed if the Special Advocate feels that lack of payment is being used to interfere with his/her conduct of the court-assigned tasks.

FORMAT II: A draw-down account is established. When the account reaches the level of $ _____ , it is brought back up to the original balance. The Special Advocate will notify the parties when that level has been reached. Any unspent monies at the end of the Special Advocate's term will be refunded.

7. We choose _____ . If Format II is chosen, the initial amount of the deposit is agreed to be _____ . We agree to pay the full amount in the following proportions: Mother _____ %, Father _____ %. If there is a disagreement as to payment proportions or format,

it will be referred back to the parties' attorneys for settlement. The work of the Special Advocate will not begin until payment proportions and format are agreed upon.

8. We understand that in addition to face-to-face time, charges will include time spent reviewing documents; drafting agreements or reports to the Court; consultations with therapists, doctors, and other service providers to the parties and their child(ren); consultations with attorneys; and court testimony, including travel time to and from court. There is no charge for brief scheduling telephone calls. There will be a charge for telephone calls from the parties that are informational or essentially therapeutic in nature. Charges for long-distance calls, copies of documents, or fax charges may be assessed by the Special Advocate if they, in his/her opinion, go beyond normal and reasonable office overhead expenses.

9. We understand that _____(professional's name)_____ reserves the right, on a session-by-session basis, to alter the payment ratio if he/she believes that one party has used the session in a disruptive way. This would include, but is not limited to, forgetting to appear at a scheduled appointment, storming out of a session before its logical conclusion, or "sandbagging" so as to undermine the Special Advocate process. He/she also reserves the right to inform us if he/she feels we are taking an inordinate amount of time to solve a relatively minor problem. We agree that the amount of time spent on a topic shall be determined by the Special Advocate.

10. We understand that _____(professional's name)_____ does not release information to the Court in the form of recommendations, evaluations, or parenting plans unless he/she has been paid prior to the release of the work. If ordered by the Court to do so, he/she will, but then pursue available means to collect the balance due.

If Mediation Is Part of the Special Advocate Role:

11. The purpose of mediation is to help parties reach a jointly approved solution to an impasse in their parenting of the child(ren). Mediation offers a safe and structured place for people to discuss their differences, come to an understanding of his/her and the other's position, and reach a solution that best serves the child(ren).

12. In mediation, all written and oral communications, negotiations, and statements made in the course of mediation are considered confidential. Since information provided in mediation will be considered by the Special Advocate in making a report to the Court (or in making an arbitration award if that is part of the Special Advocate's defined role), confidentiality is not assured. Issues raised in #3 above also cannot be kept confidential given the reporting requirement.

If Arbitration Is Part of the Special Advocate Role:

13. We intend to resolve issues through mediation as much as possible. In the event that a mutually satisfactory resolution of an impasse cannot be reached, the Special Advocate, if so authorized by the court order, may serve as an arbitrator. That is he/she will arbitrate the issue and make a decision for us based upon the communication and information we have provided. In addition, the Special Advocate or either party may also request the submission of written statements of positions and facts to the Special Advocate. Either party may then respond in writing to the other party's written statement. The Special Advocate shall then review the statements and responses and issue a written arbitration award regarding the issue. We understand and agree that we will be bound by the award of the Special Advocate.

14. We understand that either of us may request that an arbitration hearing be held.

15. In the event that a formal arbitration hearing will be held, the following procedures will be observed:

a) One week prior to the hearing on the matters to be submitted to arbitration, or at such time as designated by the Special Advocate in consultation with the parties, each parent shall submit a statement to the Special Advocate. The statement shall summarize the matters in dispute; the legal issues pending; and the legal authority supporting his or her position, if appropriate. The statement shall also list the witnesses who shall testify and a brief summary of each witness's testimony. If the Special Advocate must consult with an attorney because of the legal complexities of the issue, the cost of the consultation shall be borne by the parties. The Special Advocate does not normally deal with complicated legal issues and may refer such to an arbitrator better versed in the legal complexities of the issue.

b) The parents may choose to have the Special Advocate consult with expert witnesses such as therapists, custody/ parenting responsibility evaluators, teachers, medical providers, etc., outside of the hearing and may agree that such information be included in the information base upon which the award is determined. Unless otherwise stated by the parties, the Special Advocate assumes that the information from such consultations is to be used for the arbitration award.

c) The hearing date and time shall be determined by mutual agreement of the parties involved. Notice of the meeting shall be by U.S. mail, postage prepaid. The Special Advocate, at his/her sole discretion, may continue the hearing upon request of either parent for good cause or when both parents are in agreement as to a request to postpone. All hearings will take place in the offices of the Special Advocate unless the parties and the Special Advocate agree otherwise.

d) Either parent may provide a certified court reporter for all arbitration hearing proceedings and shall be responsible for all associated expenses for recording the hearing.

e) Either parent may be accompanied by an attorney of his/her choice. Other parties involved must be informed of this two (2) weeks in advance so they too may be accompanied by an attorney if they so wish.

16. We agree that the Special Advocate may interview and/or observe our child(ren) privately in order to develop a sense of the child(ren), his/her style, and his/her needs. We understand that the Special Advocate will avoid pressing the child(ren) to choose sides between us.

17. We understand that we may request a telephone conference between us and the Special Advocate. We agree that the conference will be held on land-line phones, not cell phones. We understand if the telephone conference is long distance or requires the services of a conference-call coordinator, the Special Advocate reserves the right to charge for those additional service fees. Such charges will be divided in proportion as defined by the Special Advocate court order, regardless of who is "on the road."

18. OTHER AGREEMENTS:

Signed this _____ day of _____ , 20 ____ .

_____   _____
Signature   Signature

_____
(Professional's Name) (Special Advocate)

16

Parenting Coordination
Follow-up Forms

Form 16–1: Status of Referral for Parenting Coordination
Form 16–2: Recommendations and Report from Parenting Coordinator
Form 16–3: Contact and Outcome Checklist for Parenting Coordination

FORM 16–1:
STATUS OF REFERRAL FOR PARENTING COORDINATION

Judge _____ Date _____

Docket Number _____ Case Name _____

❑   The parents have:

    ❑   resolved all current issues.

    ❑   resolved some issues.

    ❑   agreed to continue parent coordination to work on other issues.

    ❑   agreed to continue parent-coordination work on an as-needed basis.

    ❑   not agreed on any issues.

    ❑   agreed to no longer use a parenting coordinator.

❑   A session could not be scheduled because: _____

_____

❑   One or more parties did not attend the session: _____

_____

❑   The matter was settled prior to meeting with (Parenting Coordinator).

❑   Other _____

Comments: _____

_____

_____

_____

_____

_____

_____

Signed: _____

_____

Used with permission of Kim Willis.

FORM 16–2:
RECOMMENDATIONS AND REPORT
FROM PARENTING COORDINATOR

STATE OF _____   _____ FAMILY COURT

_____ COUNTY, SS.   DOCKET NO. _____

VS.

In a Stipulation signed by both parties and filed with the _____ _____ Family Court, it was agreed that:

1. _____ shall serve as Parenting Coordinator (PC) in the above-entitled matter for the purpose of resolving issues related to parent–child contact.

2. The PC shall assist the parties in developing a parenting plan for the child(ren). Specifically, the PC shall:

   a) Meet with each party, separately or together at his/her discretion. In addition, the PC may meet with any child(ren), persons who have relationships with the child(ren), and professionals who have provided services to the child(ren) or the parents.

   b) Make recommendations to the parties regarding parent–child contact schedules, safety issues, drop-off and pick-up arrangements, and other child-related concerns consistent with the best interests of the child(ren). The PC may also refer the parties to services in the community that are necessary to the implementation of the parenting plan and the creation of a safe environment for the child(ren). The recommendations of the PC shall be in writing with copies to the Court.

   c) If the parties reach agreement regarding a parenting plan, the PC's recommendations shall be accompanied by a signed memoranda of agreement between the parents.

d) If the parties are unable to reach agreement regarding a parenting plan, the PC shall file a recommended parenting plan with the Court. The PC's recommendations may also address the need to have certain issues heard by the Court on a contested hearing and/or the need for a home study or forensic evaluation.

e) If either party objects to the parenting plan recommended by the parent coordinator, he/she shall file written objections within ten (10) days following the filing of the PC's recommended plan. After reviewing the recommendations and the objections, the Court will schedule the matter for hearing to discuss the objections and determine whether to adopt the PC's recommendations in whole or in part.

f) Pending a court hearing, the PC is authorized to direct the parties to follow an interim parent–child contact schedule if he/she believes that this is in the best interests of the child(ren).

Based on this agreement, the PC makes the following report and recommendations to the Court on behalf of the minor child(ren):

Used with permission of Jennifer Barker, Vermont Family Court Mediation Program, Parent Coordination Services.

FORM 16–3:
CONTACT AND OUTCOME CHECKLIST
FOR PARENTING COORDINATION

STATE OF _____   _____ FAMILY COURT

_____ COUNTY, SS.   DOCKET NO. _____

VS.

Parenting Coordinator (PC) _____
was contacted on (date) _____ by (party) _____
_____ regarding stipulated/ordered dispute resolution.

❑ Parenting coordination was offered to and accepted by the parties.

❑ Parenting coordination was offered to and refused by (name of parent).

_____

❑ Parenting coordination was attempted by the parties but the dispute-resolution process was unsuccessful. Referred back to family court for hearing.

❑ Recommendation from the PC is attached.

_____   _____

Parenting Coordinator's Signature   Date

Used with permission of Jennifer Barker, Vermont Family Court Mediation Program, Parent Coordination Services.

17

Supervised Visitation

Sometimes conflict between the parents is severe enough to endanger the children physically as well as psychologically. In these cases, supervised visitation may be necessary to ensure the children's safety. Usually supervised visitation is time limited and the goal is to move to less restrictive visitation. Gauging the degree of risk is difficult. A task force in Massachusetts created a comprehensive protocol for the court to follow in providing protection for children.

Form 17–1: Supervised Visitation Risk Assessment for Judges
Form 17–2: Supervised Visitation Contract
Form 17–3: Guidelines for Moving from Supervised to Unsupervised Visitation

FORM 17–1:
SUPERVISED VISITATION RISK ASSESSMENT FOR JUDGES

It is not enough that children *be safe*, they must *feel safe* as well.

This bench guide is intended to aid the decision maker in determining when and what kind of safeguards should be in place to protect children during parent–child contact. Recognizing that decisions often need to be made before all the relevant evidence has been assembled, this outline suggests questions intended to guide the thinking of the decision maker.

Supervised Visitation Task Force

In January 1998, in recognition of the important role that supervised visitation plays in protecting families, the Honorable Sean M. Dunphy, Chief Justice of the Probate and Family Court, established a Supervised Visitation Task Force. The mission of the task force was to create a comprehensive protocol for the Court to follow when ordering supervised visitation.

The task force has worked diligently during the past year to comply with its mandate. A significant portion of this protocol is the risk-assessment guide. The guide is intended to complement and augment the earlier Domestic Violence Risk Assessment Guide. It is the hope of the task-force members that this risk assessment will improve court practices relative to the appropriate use of supervised visitation, helping families to maintain parent–child contact in a safe environment.

It is the desire and recommendation of this committee that the risk-assessment guide be reviewed within two years after implementation. Thus, this committee hopes that this document will continue to evolve.

I would like to extend a well-deserved thank-you to all the members of the task force for their willingness to give so generously of their time and talent. In addition to the task force members, this guide was reviewed by many other practitioners and mental health professionals working with these highly complex families.

—Honorable Arline S. Rotman, Chair

Members of the Supervised Visitation Task Force

CHAIR:

Honorable Arline S. Rotman, Worcester Division, Probate and Family Court Department

MEMBERS:

Honorable David G. Sacks, Hampden Division, Probate and Family Court Department

Honorable Stephen C. Steinberg, Plymouth Division, Probate and Family Court Department

Catherine C. Ayoub, Ph.D., Children and the Law Program, Massachusetts General Hospital

Sheila Brown, Assistant Chief Probation Officer, Middlesex Division, Probate and Family Court Department

Lonna Davis, Supervisor, Domestic Violence Unit, Department of Social Services

Mary M. Ferriter, MPA, JD, Administrative Office, Probate and Family Court Department

Geri S.W. Fuhrmann, Psy.D., Director Child and Family Forensic Center, University of Massachusetts Medical School

Linda Paolino Hughes, Director, New Hope Family Visitation Center

William O'Riordan, Chief Probation Officer, Hampshire Division, Probate and Family Court Department

Kathleen Nelligan, Probation Officer, Essex Division, Probate and Family Court Department

Robert B. Straus, DMH, JD, Co-chair Supervised Visitation Network

Section I. Why Use Supervised Visitation: Purpose

The Court needs to ensure the psychological, as well as the physical safety of the child. If a parent poses a risk of physical harm to the child due to such things as poor impulse control or poor parental judgment, then the need for the presence of a responsible adult during parent–child contact is obvious. The Court must still, however, assess the level of risk to determine the appropriate type of supervision.

The risk of psychological harm is more difficult to gauge. Same-aged children in similar circumstances can be affected differently as a result of factors unique to the child such as temperament, intelligence, and environment. It is therefore crucial to understand something about the particular child, in addition to the general needs of children at different ages, to make an informed decision about the need for supervision.

Many times the Court is asked to weigh the risk of harm to a child in permitting continued contact under less-than-optimum circumstances against the harm that would come from eliminating parent–child contact. This is a difficult and demanding decision facing the Court. Professional supervision is not a realistic option for all cases, and in many cases is not needed. The Court must decide when it is appropriate to allow a nonprofessional supervisor to oversee parent–child contact. When no supervisor is available, the Court will have to determine whether or not supervision is essential to the child's safety or are other protective mechanisms sufficient. In some circumstances, the Court may utilize visitation orders that provide for a supervised or restricted transfer or other restricting measures to address the safety concerns.

There will be instances, however, when even professionally supervised contact cannot protect the child from further trauma. In those cases, the Court should suspend contact until such time as the Court is satisfied that the physical or psychological safety of the child is no longer in jeopardy.

Supervised visitation is not intended to be a permanent solution to a family's crisis, but rather it is an interim measure. It is a temporary remedy to provide the child with safe access to the parent. In most instances, a family should be able to move to less restrictive and then unsupervised contact within a reasonable time frame. In other cases, the court may find that continuation of the parent–child relationship is not in the child's best interest.

The ultimate purpose of supervised visitation is to protect a child from physical and/or psychological harm while preserving the parent–child relationship whenever possible.

Section II. What Is Supervised Visitation: Types and Considerations

1. Supervised Transfer

The exchange of a child between a custodial party and a noncustodial party that is carried out under the supervision of a suitable third party. The remainder of the parent–child contact is not supervised. The purpose of supervised transfer is to keep high-conflict parents separate and to provide children a neutral presence and emotional support to ease difficult transitions. Supervision of transfers may not provide adequate protection in domestic violence cases.

Consider ordering supervised transfers when:

- there is little or no concern about the capacity of the visiting parent to take care of the child;
- there is significant risk of direct conflict between parents at times of transition;
- a child has difficulty with transitions (separation issues and/or loyalty conflicts);
- concern exists that a custodial parent may interfere with visits;
- there is need to monitor the mental or physical status of the visiting parent before allowing a visit to proceed, for example, when that parent has a history of mental illness or substance abuse.

Note: An order to exchange the children at a police station is not a supervised transfer because there is no person actually supervising the exchange. An exchange at a police station should be used sparingly and only when there is no other alternative. Such exchanges do not meet the purposes of a supervised transfer and the wrong message about the role of the police is conveyed to the child.

2. Supervised Visitation

Supervised visitation is contact between a parent and one or more children in the presence of a suitable third party. This third party observes, listens, and intervenes if necessary to protect the child(ren). The purpose of supervised visitation is to protect a child from physical or emotional harm during a visit by observing, limiting, or modifying the visiting parent's behavior, as well as to provide factual observations of what happens during visits and to protect all parties during exchanges.

Consider ordering supervised visitation:

- when risk exists that a visiting parent may abuse a child physically or sexually;
- in partner-abuse situations; to protect against abuse, manipulation, or inappropriate questioning of child(ren) by a visiting parent; and to provide safety during transitions;
- when there is a danger of false allegations about a visiting parent's behavior during visit;
- when a child is refusing to visit;
- when separated parents are in protracted high conflict and the child(ren) is (are) showing symptoms of intense loyalty conflict and/or there is concern that a parent may speak negatively about the other parent or manipulate the child(ren);
- when there are concerns about a visiting parent's ability to care adequately for a child during visits due to mental illness, substance abuse, inexperience, or other dysfunction;
- to provide factual information that will assist in evaluation when there are unresolved questions about any of the above issues.

Note: All supervised visitation does not require the same level of vigilance. Generally, a supervisor remains close enough to observe and hear all interactions. If there is low risk that a parent will manipulate or inappropriately question a child, supervision may be less vigilant with a supervisor present but remaining at some distance from the parent and child. When a family is ready to move towards unsupervised contact, by parental agreement or order a supervisor may leave the visiting parent and child unattended for a portion of the visit.

3. Closely Supervised Visitation in High-Risk Cases

Closely Supervised Visitation is contact between a noncustodial party and one or more children in the presence of an experienced professional supervisor. This supervisor is experienced in anticipating and managing difficult situations. The supervisor must remain close enough throughout each visit to hear all interactions and to intervene if necessary at any moment. The presence of a particular risk of harm to the child, including such things as risks of violence, sexual abuse, gross mental or emotional abuse, and/or child abduction distinguish the situation as high risk. The purpose of closely supervised visitation is to provide an extra measure of security when there are special risks.

Consider ordering closely supervised visitation when a high risk is present such as:

- a history of severe domestic violence or particularly high inter-parental conflict: in these cases the child may be traumatized and hypersensitive. There may be a need to closely monitor all conversations and the child's reactions;
- a particularly high risk exists of abduction or abuse of a child;

Note: It may be appropriate to initiate closely supervised visitation during periods of crisis, then to return to regular supervised visitation.

4. Supportive Supervised Visitation

Supportive Supervised Visitation is contact between a noncustodial party and one or more children in the presence of a suitable third person, in which the supervisor, in addition to providing observation and protection for the child, is actively involved in parent education and modeling positive, appropriate behavior to foster the parent–child relationship. The purpose of supportive supervised visitation is to improve the relationship between parent and child, to improve parenting skills of the visiting parent, and to provide reassurance to the child(ren) and to the custodial parent.

Consider ordering supportive supervised visitation when:

- there is low conflict and a noncustodial parent has limited parenting skills and/or has had little or no prior relationship with the child, as in "paternity" cases;

- a parent's ability is impaired because of mental retardation;
- when a child (or custodial parent) needs to overcome fears and anxieties about beginning or resuming contact.

Note: This intervention actively encourages the parent–child relationship. Unless the goal of improving the parent–child relationship is supported by both parents, the intervention can be seen as one-sided: supporting the noncustodial parent. A child could experience loyalty conflicts and the custodial parent could be alienated from the process.

5. Therapeutic Supervision

Therapeutic supervision involves active interventions by the supervisor to help establish a relationship or to ameliorate problems in the parent–child relationship. It is a combination of supervised visitation and parent–child therapy, provided by a licensed mental health professional. The purpose of therapeutic supervision is to cause change in emotional issues affecting the adult(s) and/or child(ren) who are having supervised visits.

Consider ordering therapeutic supervision when:

- the child(ren) is (are) severely distressed by supervised visits or refusing to visit, as an alternative to suspending or terminating contact;
- an inexperienced parent needs help understanding his/her child's moods and emotional needs;
- a child is asking questions about sensitive issues (like prior abuse of a parent or child or a parent's affair) that need discussion, but a supervisor without mental health training is not equipped to handle;
- visits under supervision seem stuck and there is no movement toward ending supervision or terminating contact.

Note: Therapeutic supervision may be most effective if used in combination with individual therapeutic work with the parents to resolve issues of conflict over the children.

6. Off-Site Supervision

Off-site supervision involves any of the above types of supervision that is not limited to a confined location. In appropriate situations, either as a transition from more restrictive supervision or to allow for a more natural parent–child relationship, visits may occur in a public place such as a mall, park, or museum. The purpose of off-site supervision is to make possible longer contacts (two hours or more) and give visiting parents both more freedom (less structure) and more responsibility; also to make possible professional or nonprofessional supervision where no protected center is available.

Consider permitting off-site supervision when:

- a move towards unsupervised contact is being considered, as an intermediate step;
- supervision must continue for a long time, as in sexual abuse cases, when risk is low but ongoing protection is necessary because of potential recurrence of abuse.

Note: High-risk cases may be supervised off site, but only if the security precautions match the risk, including such measures as supervisors having cellular phones and careful plans to avoid parent contact at transitions.

Section III. When to Use Supervised Visitation

A. Factors to Consider to Determine Parent–Child Contact

Consideration of the following factors can provide valuable data to inform decision making. Recognizing that these decisions must often be made on the basis of limited information, consideration of the following factors can focus the decision maker's inquiry and make this task less daunting.

Factors to consider regarding each child:

1. *Age* of the child

   - Younger children are more vulnerable, physically and psychologically.

- Preverbal children cannot report their experiences and feelings.
- Separation anxiety is heightened for 1- to 5-year-olds so a known supervisor is particularly important.
- Preteens and teens appropriately want some voice in decisions affecting them. Where possible their views regarding parent–child contact orders should be independently obtained.

2. *Siblings*

- The presence of a sibling during the parent–child contact can be a strong protective factor and mitigate possible psychological stress.

3. Child's *behavioral and psychological reactions* to contact with the noncustodial parent.

- A child who demonstrates symptoms of ongoing distress should be considered vulnerable.
- Symptoms can signify a level of stress that exceeds the child's capacity to cope.
- The following symptoms are indicative of problems and may be indicative of difficulties stemming from contact with the noncustodial parent:
  a) Emotional
     1. depression, i.e., irritability, sadness
     2. anger
     3. fearfulness
  b) Physical
     1. stomachaches
     2. headaches
  c) Behavioral
     1. aggression
     2. withdrawal
     3. regression
     4. risk-taking behaviors
     5. problems with peer relationships
     6. school-related problems

- The existence of a cluster of these symptoms reported in *connection with contact with the noncustodial parent* should be a red flag for the Court to consider ordering supervised contact.
- In considering a report of symptoms, questions should be asked about the duration and intensity. For example, a 4-year-old who cries when leaving the primary caretaker but plays happily within fifteen minutes and is not otherwise symptomatic is not concerning. However, a 4-year-old who cries continuously, does not accept comfort, and then is withdrawn and clingy at home raises the level of concern.
- Consideration should also be given to other factors in the child's life, including the child's relationship with the custodial parent and the level of conflict between the parents.

4. *Quality of the relationship* between child and the residential parent or other adult

  - Children who can share their experiences with a nurturant caretaker they trust fare better than children who only have their own limited resources on which to rely. Having one trusted and caring adult can make a difference in a child's capacity to withstand stress.

5. *Quality of the relationship* between the child and the noncustodial parent

  - Suspending, limiting, or allowing contact with a noncustodial parent who has been involved in the child's life will often have a different impact on the child than the same order for a child who has had less prior contact.

6. *Overall functioning* of the child

  - A child who is functioning well is likely to be more resilient than a child who is doing poorly. A child who is functioning well is more likely to have internal strengths to withstand the stresses associated with a supervised visitation case.
  - Consider if the child is having difficulty in any of the following areas:

a. academically
b. socially
c. emotionally
d. medically
e. developmentally

For example, a child with learning disabilities and chronic asthma may be more vulnerable than a healthy child who does well in school.

7. *Therapeutic treatment* for the child

- The existence of a therapist for the child can be an important safeguard, since the therapist is a mandated reporter for abuse or neglect. He/she can provide a voice for the child and additional information regarding the child's experience of the visits.

Factors to consider regarding each parent:

1. *Takes responsibility* for the situation leading to the need for supervision

- A parent who is able to acknowledge his/her part in a situation is more likely to be able to consider the child's experience than a parent who projects blame onto others. Of greatest concern is a parent who believes that the child is responsible for the situation that led to a request for supervision.

2. *Awareness of the impact* of the negative behavior on the child

- Unfortunately, many parents have difficulty imagining that their children's experience may be different than their own. The father who, when asked how he thought sexual abuse affected his 9-year-old daughter, replied, "If I'm okay, she's okay" or the robber who could not understand his son's sense of shame are examples of this. Parents who cannot empathize with their children, that is, cannot see the world through their eyes, are less likely to be aware of their child's needs and present a greater risk of harm to the child.

3. *Therapeutic treatment* for either or both parents

- It is important to ascertain what kind of therapy the parent(s) is currently receiving and whether that treatment has been successful.
- Obtaining evaluation and treatment for a problem is an important step towards ameliorating the problem. Factors to consider in evaluating the prognosis of the parent's treatment include:
  a. motivation of the parent
  b. parent's amenability to treatment
  c. skill of treatment provider
  d. seriousness of problem
  e. frequency, consistency, and type of treatment

4. *Behavior of parent*

- If a person's baseline behavior over time has been nonprob-lematic, and concerns have only recently arisen, then one can feel more confident that the parent's functioning will improve once the current crisis has subsided. For example, a mother who held a steady job with no past psychiatric hospitalizations who gets intoxicated and makes a serious suicide attempt when she learns of her husband's affair will likely present less of a risk once she stabilizes than a mother who has struggled with depression and drinking for ten years.
- If domestic violence is the concern and the parent has a history of violent outbursts, then precautions need to be taken to provide for the psychological and physical safety of the child.

5. Realistic view of the *safety needs* of the child

- The importance of this factor varies with the age and ability of the child to protect him-/herself. A parent with little or no parenting experience may not appreciate the need for constant supervision of a toddler.

- A parent with impaired judgment as a result of substance abuse or mental illness may need supervision until the problem(s) is (are) controlled or the child is old enough to be educated to understand the parent's limitations. A child with special needs, such as a 3-year-old with a peanut allergy or a 10-year-old with attention deficit disorder may require the skills of a parent with better-developed judgment.

6. Availability of *parental supports* and/or resources

- A parent must be willing and able to seek help when needed.
- The existence of family, friends, church, and therapists can all be important.
- An inexperienced parent living with his/her own parent who recognizes the need for assistance does not present the risk that a similarly inexperienced parent does who cannot or will not rely on the support and assistance of family members and/or responsible friends.

7. Custodial parent's *level of fear*

- Children are attuned to the emotions of their primary parent.
- If a primary parent is truly frightened (and has a reasonable basis for this fear) by the prospect of a child having contact with the other parent, then that parent's fear will be conveyed to the child. This will interfere with the child's ability to enjoy the contact with the other parent. An order that provides appropriate protections can reassure the primary parent and allow him/her to better support the child's relationship with the other parent.

8. Parent's *criminal history*

- It is well known that the best predictor of future behavior is past behavior. Knowledge about a parent's past wrongful behavior can help one more accurately predict future behavior.

- Particular concern should be given to recent indications of violent crime and/or substance abuse or any reports of kidnaping or child molestation.

9. *Other factors* that might increase the risk to the child

   - Involvement of extended family members who exacerbate the hostility between the parties
   - A parent's history of childhood trauma, which may bring unresolved past issues into the current situation
   - While respecting divergent cultural and religious values, consideration of society's accepted standards of parental behavior

Factors to consider regarding the family

- The existence of *additional family stressors* such as a recent job loss, financial loss, a recent death, or serious illness can create greater risks for the child. While these stressors exist, a parent may have diminished parenting capacity, which can affect a child's coping ability.

B. Circumstances Suggesting the Need for Supervised Contact

The following circumstances most often present situations that may be appropriate for Court-ordered supervised contact:

1. parent with minimal prior contact or parent wishing reconnection after prolonged visitation interruption

2. parenting skills and/or cognitive deficiencies

3. parental conflict without violence

4. visitation refusal by child or custodial parent interference with visitation

5. parental mental illness and/or substance abuse

6. partner abuse

7. physical abuse of child

8. sexual abuse of child

9. threat of abduction

In addition to the general factors listed on the preceding pages, supplemental factors may need to be considered in ascertaining the need for supervised contact and the level of risk for each particular circumstance. The following outline suggests questions to ask to define the parameters appropriate for each case. In some cases, more than one circumstance may apply.

I. Parent with Minimal Prior Contact or Parent Wishing Reconnection after Prolonged Visitation Interruption

FACTORS TO CONSIDER:

1. About the *nature of the lack of contact* or contact interruption

   - What are the reasons for or circumstances surrounding the lack of contact or contact interruption?
   - Have the reasons for the lack of contact or contact interruption been documented?
   - What is the frequency and duration of contact interruption?

2. About the *child*

   - What is the child's understanding of the no-contact period?
   - What is the child's view of restoring or initiating contact?

3. About the *parent with minimal or no contact*

   - Is he/she in treatment? What is the treatment? Is this the reason for lack of contact?
   - Did that parent have the opportunity for contact?

4. About the *other parent*

   - How does this parent view resuming/increasing contact?

II. Parenting Skills and/or Cognitive Deficiencies

FACTORS TO CONSIDER:

1. About the *nature of alleged deficiency* in parenting skill and/or cognitive processes

   - What is the nature of the alleged deficiency?
   - Has the deficiency been documented? What is the parent's presentation?
   - What are the frequency and duration of difficulties?
   - Are they global or specific to certain areas of functioning?
   - What has been or is the impact of alleged deficiency on the child(ren)?

2. About the *parent with alleged deficiency*

   - Is the parent aware of his/her limitation?
   - Has his/her deficiency led to neglect?
   - What efforts, if any, has the parent made to ameliorate the deficiency?

3. About the *other parent*

   - How is he/she around the child's ongoing care?
   - Does this parent have adequate skills/cognitive processing?
   - What is this parent's understanding of and ability to support a relationship between the child and the parent with the deficiency?

III. Parental Conflict without Violence

FACTORS TO CONSIDER:

1. About the *nature of alleged conflict*

   - What is the nature of the alleged conflict?
   - Intermittent? Continuous? Specific-issue related?

- Has the conflict been documented?
- Frequency, duration, and intensity of the conflict?

2. About the alleged parental conflict (consider for *each parent*)

- How angry is he/she?
- Are others (e.g., family, friends) supporting the conflict ("community warfare")?

3. About the *noncustodial parent*

- Is there a danger that the parent will continue the verbal assault and/or degradation of the other parent through the child?

4. About the *child*

- Is the child extraordinarily sensitive?
- What is the child's behavioral and psychological reaction to conflict?

Note: In many instances of parental conflict without violence, a supervised transfer that protects the child from further exposure to parental conflict will suffice.

IV. Visitation Refusal by Child or Custodial Parent Interference with Visitation

FACTORS TO CONSIDER:

1. About the *nature of refusal or interference*

- What are stated reasons for refusal/interference?
- Any collaborating information for the stated concerns?
- Duration of refusal/interference?
- Frequency of refusal/interference (some or all of the time)?

2. About the *child*

- Are all the children having disrupted visitation (if more than one child)?

- Has the child been exposed to parental conflict?
- Has the quality of the relationship with a parent changed?
- Is the child in treatment? Is this issue being addressed with the child's therapist?

3. About the *alleged interfering parent*

- What is parent's view?
- Is parent able to differentiate her/his view from that of the child?
- Does parent have any insight into how the behavior affects the parent–child relationship?

4. About the *other (noncustodial) parent*

- What is parent's view?
- Is she/he able to differentiate her/his own view from that of the children?
- How does he/she respond to visitation refusal or obstruction?
- Is this parent amenable to maintaining minimal contact at a level tolerable for the child until therapeutic work can be done with the child?

V. Parental Mental Illness and/or Substance Abuse

FACTORS TO CONSIDER:

1. About the *nature of alleged mental illness and/or substance abuse*

- What is the nature of the alleged mental illness and/or substance abuse?
- Has the illness or abuse been documented? What is its presentation?
- What are the frequency and duration of illness or substance abuse?

2. About the *alleged mentally ill and/or substance-abusing parent*

- Is he/she in treatment? What is the treatment? What is the effectiveness of the treatment? How long has treatment been ongoing?

- Is the alleged mentally ill and/or substance-abusing parent now stable? If so, for how long? What, if any, pattern of stability/decompensation has been exhibited by the parent?
- What is the quality of the mentally ill parent's parenting skills?

3. About the *other parent*

- Are these issues (e.g., substance abuse, mental illness) in this parent as well?
- Does this parent understand mental illness/substance abuse issues?

4. About the *child*

- Is the child old enough or of sufficient intellectual development to be educated about the signs and nature of the illness?
- What has been the impact on the child of the mental illness/substance abuse?

VI. *Partner Abuse*

FACTORS TO CONSIDER:

1. About the *nature of alleged abuse*

- What is the nature of the alleged abuse?
- What is the evidence for the alleged abuse?
- Is there a history of controlling or abusive behavior?
- What is the frequency? What is the most recent episode?
- What is the most severe incident?
- Was this an isolated incident?

2. About the *child*

- Has the child witnessed, heard, or seen the violence or aftermath?

- Has the child been used to further control the parent?
- Has the child been hurt or neglected?
- Is the Department of Social Services involved?
- Has the child intervened to protect the abused parent?
- Has the child aligned with the abusive parent?

3. About the *alleged abusive parent*

- Is the abusive parent claiming to be the victim?
- Does the parent have a history of violence?
- Does he/she acknowledge abusive behavior? Is he/she in treatment for abusive behavior? If so, what is the effectiveness?

4. About the *alleged victim*

- Is parent currently safe?
- Has parent sustained injuries?
- Can he/she separate his/her needs from those of children?
- History of prior victimization, mental illness, substance abuse?

VII. *Physical Abuse of Child*

FACTORS TO CONSIDER:

1. About the *nature of alleged abuse*

- What is the nature of the alleged abuse/neglect?
- Has abuse been documented?
- Frequency and duration of physical abuse or neglect?
- When did abuse allegedly last occur?

2. About the *child*

- Has the child been traumatized? Is the child suffering from post-traumatic stress disorder?
- Has the child become aggressive or withdrawn?

3. About the *allegedly abusive parent*

- Does the parent have insight into how the abuse occurred?

- Does the parent have an understanding of the impact of the abuse on the child?
- Does the parent have a history of violent behavior toward others?
- Are there cultural issues influencing the parent's use of physical discipline that rises to the level of abuse?
- Does this parent understand the need to protect the child?

VIII. Sexual Abuse of Child

FACTORS TO CONSIDER:

1. About the *nature of alleged abuse*

   - What is the nature of the alleged abuse?
   - What is the evidence for the alleged abuse?
   - Frequency and duration of the sexual abuse?
   - When did abuse allegedly last occur?
   - Is Department of Social Services involved?
   - Has an evaluation been completed or is there one pending? Might this investigation be complicated or negatively impacted by contact with the alleged perpetrator?

2. About the *child*

   - How was the target child/children impacted?
   - What is the child's current need for protection?
   - Has the child articulated a wish to see or not to see the alleged perpetrator?
   - Does the child associate any particular place or nonperpetrating person with the abuse?

3. About the *other parent*

   - Is this parent a survivor of sexual abuse or in other ways vulnerable?

4. About the *allegedly abusive parent*

   - Does the parent have insight into how the abuse occurred?

- Does the parent have an understanding of the impact of the abuse on the child?
- Is there a pending criminal action against the parent?
- If the parent is in treatment has he/she developed a plan for preventing a re-offense?

IX. Threat of Abduction

FACTORS TO CONSIDER:

1. About the *nature of alleged threat*

   - Evidence for and nature of threat?
   - Frequency and history of threats to abduct?
   - If not a direct threat, what led parent to be concerned? Who reported the threat and to whom?

2. About the *child*

   - Has the child(ren) been exposed to threats before? What does he/she know now?
   - How easily transportable is the child (younger, healthy children are easier to conceal and less conspicuous when moving about)?

3. About the *alleged threatening parent*

   - Does he/she have the resources to carry out the threat (such as, a place to go, ties to another area)?
   - Does he/she have citizenship in another country?
   - Does he/she recognize the importance of the other parent in the child's life (can they see how or why both parents should play a role in the child's future)?
   - Does he/she have a social network that would provide emotional support and financial assistance to the parent?
   - Has he/she liquidated assets, withdrawn large amounts of cash (bank withdrawals or cash advances on credit cards)?
   - Does the parent have a history of contempt for authority?

- Does the parent have paranoid, irrational beliefs and behaviors or psychotic delusions?

4. About the *litigation*

- Has there been an allegation of sexual abuse or physical abuse that the alleged threatening parent feels was not taken seriously by the legal authorities?[1]

---

1. Research has shown that mothers and fathers are equally likely to abduct their child. However, when no custody order is in place, the father is more likely to be the abductor. After the court has issued a formal custody order, the mother is more likely to be the abductor.

Used with permission of the Honorable Sean M. Dunphy, Chief Justice of Probate and Family Court in Massachusetts.

FORM 17-2:
SUPERVISED VISITATION CONTRACT

We offer professionally supervised visitations for the purpose of allowing a child to interact with his/her mother or father in a physically safe and emotionally caring environment. These visitations are utilized to allow the child to become reacquainted with a parent; to determine if and how an abusive parent can have a positive role in the child's life; to provide the parents with better parenting skills; and decrease the impact of parent alienation or triangulation when it has occurred.

We believe that, in the majority of cases, children benefit from contact with both parents. We believe when children are deprived of contact with a parent, they often feel confused, guilty, and angry. These children often try to imitate the behavior of the absent parent and can develop very low self-esteem.

Many of these cases involve situations where a parent has been abusive to the child or the other parent. We believe that abuse or high conflict is destructive to a child's sense of security and ability to be successful with friends, academics, and extracurricular activities. Therapeutic visitations assess the cause and severity of the conflict and develop a long-term plan for what role the parent will have with the child. It is the goal of these visitations to allow children to have contact with the parent while also looking at ways to reduce conflict and creating safety for everyone.

It is our experience that in high-conflict situations, *both* parents need to work hard to improve their way of interacting with the ex-spouse and the children. Research clearly indicates that these children are at high risk to have long-term problems during adolescence and adulthood unless the stress in their life is reduced significantly.

For this to be a positive experience for the child, we ask that both parents be willing to meet with the therapist when requested to provide data and feedback, to learn how to reduce stress in the child's life, to learn what are typical ways that children react to a divorce, and to develop more appropriate parenting behavior.

Our fee for supervised visitation is $ _____ per hour; our fee for therapeutic visitation is $ _____ per hour. The therapist/observer will help assess what services are needed. Besides the actual visit, we also bill when we meet with one of the parents after the visit to debrief and instruct; for phone time; for writing reports; and for time spent individually with the child.

Generally, the supervised visits follow a three-step process. The first step is complete supervision. These visits begin in the office and can move outside to parks, events, shopping malls, and activity centers as the supervisor deems that it is prudent.

During the second phase, the parent and child meet for longer periods of time (two to four hours) that are still supervised. This phase begins when there has not been any observable problems in the one-hour visits and the child is feeling comfortable with the parent (usually after two to four months).

The third phase is initiated when the observer believes that there is relatively little risk that the supervised parent will triangulate the child, engage in any dangerous or illegal activity (i.e., drinking and driving, interrogating the child, starting fights, etc.), or put the child at risk from negligence or abuse (i.e., emotional, physical, or sexual).

During the third phase, the child is allowed to have unsupervised visitation with the noncustodial parent, but the two must still check in for monitoring after the visit. Usually the unsupervised time begins with one hour and increases in response to the child's level of comfort.

During this time, the observer is developing a long-term time-share model that addresses the developmental needs of the child, the limitations and strengths of each parent, and the existing relationship between the parents.

When it appears that the child can consistently spend unsupervised time with the parent without being triangulated or abused, then the observer will write a recommendation to the Court reviewing the progress of the case and stating his/her recommendations for long-term time share. If overnights are a possibility, that will also be addressed in the recommendations.

Listed below are some of the basic rules and information that the parents need to know:

1. When either parent or both are involved in a support group or therapy, there usually are fewer problems and the child does better in developing a positive relationship with both parents.

We will make recommendations that a parent get into therapy or counseling if it is crucial to the success of the visits.

2. Supervised visitation is a delicate balance of opposing forces. We want to make sure the child is safe, and we also want a natural unsupervised visitation schedule to be developed when appropriate. Often this means that one parent wants to slow down the process and the other parent is frustrated that the process is not going fast enough. Our goal is to continue to assess what is in the "best interests of the child."

3. *NEITHER* the content and process of the meetings or the conversations with the observer *IS CONFIDENTIAL*; THE OBSERVATIONS WILL BE MADE KNOWN TO THE COURTS, the GAL, and the child's therapist.

4. Since the Counselor is responsible to the Courts for the physical and emotional well-being of the child, it is imperative that the Counselor have the final say in any disagreements with the parent being supervised. Any resistance to complying with the counselor's requests is grounds for terminating all future visits at _____. Any disagreements with the counselor shall be discussed after the child has left the building. There are times when a special appointment will need to be set to discuss the differences and concerns.

I have read the above pages concerning supervised and therapeutic visitations. All of my questions and concerns have been addressed satisfactorily; I realize I have the right to consult with my attorney before signing this form. I realize that if I believe the services rendered at _____ are unethical or unprofessional, I have the right to present my case to the State Board of Grievances, located at _____.

I am aware that the service I am receiving is for _____ _____ and the cost is _____ /hour.

I realize that the charges by the therapist for Court appearance is $ _____ per hour (portal to portal) and must be paid seven days prior to the Court hearing. I realize that missed appointments are charged at the full rate unless the therapist is notified at least forty-eight hours in advance, a medical emergency occurred, or inclement weather has created hazardous road conditions. I am aware that the current laws in _____(state)_____ allow the therapist to charge up to _____ times the amount of any returned check and that services may be suspended or discontinued if the account is not kept current. I am aware that services are to be paid at the time of service unless otherwise agreed upon in writing.

I, _____ , agree to pay _____ % of the costs incurred at _____ plus 100% of the Court costs if I require the therapist's presence at Court.

_____   _____

Parent's Signature   Date

I, _____ , agree to pay _____ % of the costs incurred at _____ plus 100% of the Court costs if I require the therapist's presence at Court.

_____   _____

Parent's Signature   Date

_____

Used with permission of Robert S. Hovenden.

FORM 17–3:
GUIDELINES FOR MOVING FROM SUPERVISED
TO UNSUPERVISED VISITATION

For the parent who shows good progress, some signs of recovery, and who has consistently come for the visits for 3 to 6 months, design a series of progressive steps toward less supervised visitation, shaping to a developmentally appropriate, unsupervised schedule.

Block 1:   One-hour visitation with supervisor in the room. This phase should last twelve weeks to demonstrate commitment to recovery, visitation, and safety to the child(ren).

Block 2:   Move to two hours at _____ (visitation center) _____ with the supervisor on the premises but not in the room. Ideally, a way to spot check the visit is to walk into the room unexpectedly or to listen in on audio or video monitors. Supervisor, alone with the child(ren), should debrief him/her on how it went.

Block 3:   Go out in public to engage in developmentally appropriate fun time together that healthy families engage in such as eating out, sports events as participants or spectators, and recreational activities. The supervisor will accompany and debrief the child(ren) after the visit. To contain the cost, a student, a safety monitor, or a trusted friend or relative can supervise, but debriefing must be with a trained mental health professional.

Block 4:   Go out in the real world and the parent demonstrates functioning as a healthy parent would, which is managing their own impulses, keeping their child(ren) safe, setting limits, and modeling good problem solving. Examples would be the grocery store with limits on what the child(ren) can have and how he/she is to behave, a toy store to buy a birthday present for a friend with a limit on a small gift for the child(ren), or another idea that would show some mutuality and reciprocity would be that they design something they both would enjoy and that would be appropriate to the age of the child(ren). The Safety Monitor is still going along on the visits and the supervisor debriefs.

Block 5: Parent and child(ren) get to go out alone, initially, on a two-hour visit. Supervisor debriefs after the visit. If all goes well for approximately three visits, visits can move to a half day, a full day, and, finally, a full day with an overnight. But all visits continue to be debriefed after the visit.

Block 6: Parent and children move into developmentally appropriate visitation according to the age of the child. Younger siblings can progress faster if accompanied by an older sibling to whom the child(ren) is well bonded. These rules apply from two years and older. The exception is infants who need specialized planning. Weekly or every two weeks the child meets with the supervisor to process the visitation and monitor the progress.

Block 7: The final phase is to drop the monitoring, making sure the child has a way to access the supervisor, should there be any deterioration, renewed fears, or concerns.

Realistically, this whole process should span a period from 12 to 18 months. One mistake will be a warning and will be processed and corrected while visitation remains at the same level. With the second mistake, visitation reverts to a more structured phase commensurate with the severity of the mistake.

Each phase lasts 6 to 12 weeks at the discretion of the supervisor.

Used with permission of Nancy Gary, Psy.D.

18

Parting Thoughts

Our goals with this book have been to describe the clients one is likely to work with as a Parenting Coordinator (PC), to provide guidelines for how to define one's role as a PC, and to offer a "heads up" as to the practical issues for which to prepare. There are two other areas of importance: knowing one's role in the legal system and taking care of oneself.

We assume that many readers of this book will be attorneys and mediators, and many others will be mental health professionals. Of these mental health professionals, many will be making a transition from providing therapy and psychological evaluations to working within a court system where the ground rules are very different. It takes a period of adjustment to get used to working within the court system, particularly if one has been accustomed to the closed and usually confidential confines of the therapist's office. One must go through a number of mind-set changes. These have been described in excellent detail elsewhere (Greenberg and Shuman 1997). We shall highlight PC-pertinent issues below.

- **A PC is often responsible to the court.** Normally in psychotherapy one is responsible to only the client. The client makes the therapist choice and decides whether to continue or drop out of psychotherapy. In Colorado, for instance, a licensed therapist is required by law to inform a client that he or she may continue therapy or drop out even if the therapist is urging them to continue therapy. A PC may or may not be court appointed, have the children as his or her clients, and may be required to make periodic reports to the court as to the progress of the high-conflict couple. As you have seen in the sample contracts in Chapters 11, 12, and 13, dropping a PC is not an easy task. The reason for this is that a high-conflict couple or person will often tend to want to drop a PC as soon as they feel that the PC is on the other person's side because of a ruling the PC made. This may even happen within the first month or so of beginning work! The PC has a great deal of power because of the constraints for dropping a PC. So, even though the therapeutic relationship is in many ways under the control of the client, the PC relationship is not. This changes the relationship between PC and client rather radically. In therapy, one expects candor from a client because this is "his or her process." In PC work, there will be a much greater tendency to manipulate and "play to the balcony," so as to "win" and because the PC cannot be left easily. Further, the focus of the PC is on the needs of the children and only secondarily on the desires of the parents. High-conflict parents can find this troublesome.
- **PC work cannot guarantee privacy.** In therapy, except for sexual/physical abuse or danger to oneself or others, a therapist does not reveal anything about treatment without the express permission of the client. While the issue of confidentiality has been softened somewhat by the requirements of managed care, generally speaking, the client controls who knows what about their treatment issues. In

PC work, the content and statements made in mediation are usually protected in court. Experience shows that when issues are contested, and particularly if an arbitration award follows, behaviors and issues in the mediation portion of the PC's work are likely to be revealed in court. One of the authors, for instance, was told in court that although he did not have to reveal statements made by the clients in mediation, he did have to testify to his impressions of the clients as they mediated. Further, because arbitration awards are often made using the database gathered in mediation, behavior and issues raised in mediation then become permeable. A PC must be comfortable with the relative lack of confidentiality and warn the mediation-arbitration client at the outset that it cannot be *guaranteed* even though the PC has made every effort to assure confidentiality.

- **A PC is both judgmental and detached.** While a PC is empathic and objective, as is a therapist, the role shifts when a PC must make a judgment about what the child needs versus what the parents want. A PC remains dispassionate and neutral so as not to be swept onto one side or the other of the parental conflict. A therapist tends to join with his client to see the world from his/her point of view, a stance aided by no one else in the room to provide contradictory evidence. There may be a need to persuade the parties that the PC is being fair, even when making an unpopular decision. Finally, the PC focuses on parties not present: the children. In fact, it is the focus on the children's best interests with respect to their needs that often contributes to the parents' trust of the PC despite unpopular decisions. A particular challenge to a PC, particularly if he or she comes from an "emphasize neutrality" background of psychotherapy, arises from having to make a child-focused decision when one parent's stance places the PC in the position of deciding "against" a parent.

It is doubly difficult if it appears as if the parent who "wins" is being reinforced for acting-out behavior, such as when a PC agrees that a child should not see R-rated horror movies just after a parent has withheld visitation for that very reason.

- **Problem solving is the PC's major task.** The familiar therapeutic process of modifying an individual's psychodynamics (although that would be a nice outcome) shifts to managing a dispute about the children — *and moving on.* So there is a movement from broad psychodynamic issues (as in therapy) to concrete problem solving. Further, a PC sets strict requirements for acceptable communication behavior so as to minimize the demonizing by one parent of the other or reducing problem solving to a shambles by screaming, yelling, and/or storming out of the offfice. Unlike a therapist, who moves to work through and resolve the issues, a PC more often labels and acknowledges such functioning and moves on.

- **A PC deals with information from a wide array of sources.** A therapist usually knows reality through his or her client's eyes. We have all probably seen therapists who forget that they know reality only from their client's perspective. An all-too-frequent example is a therapist who recommends custody fall to his/her client when he/she knows the other parent only through what the client has told them. For the PC there is more emphasis on solution, resolution, and outcome than there is on a single perspective of the truth. That is not to say that a PC will not be constantly pressed by each client to accept his or her particular version of "The Truth." High-conflict parents almost universally lack the ability to self-observe. They can spend endless hours trying to convince the other parent, and often the PC, that their version of the truth is The Truth! In this task, they often have the true dedication of a nineteenth-century missionary converting the heathen. A signal for this kind of focus is when a client will insist the PC function as a disciplinarian and punish the other parent for imagined or real transgressions. In our experience, the mind-set of punishment should assiduously be avoided. It only escalates the fight.

- **The goal of a PC is to seek a solution that will minimally harm the child.** The goal of a therapist is to help the client by working through issues within the therapeutic relationship. It is often the relationship of unconditional positive regard that helps the client let go of old behaviors and risk something new. A PC functions to narrow and redefine the relationship between the couple in conflict to focus only on the business of co-parenting. This involves reframing extraneous and excessively negative comments into a specific, defined area of problem solving.

- **A PC's basic outcome measurement is to reduce or remove conflict.** A therapist's basic outcome measurement is whether the client is free of his/her old symptoms and is happier. Ironically, if a PC has both parents very angry at him, but not fighting over the children, success is achieved. A PC's job is not to rearrange individual psyches, although that is a wonderful fringe benefit if achieved. In a sense, the PC rearranges the transactional relationship between two warring parents, but not their interior psyches. The shift from "cure" to "containment" is a hard one for a therapist. It is also difficult to shift from making "The Right" decision to making a good decision. A right decision is the one that makes the problem go away forever. A good decision is one that solves the problem and lets the parents move on. A good decision stops the conflict between the parties but does not rearrange their psyches. In fact, a PC will often manage the process much better than he or she will the outcome; this is all a PC is supposed to do. Although the outcome may not be ideal, the process was orderly, nondestructive, noninflammatory, and fair.

- **The PC's time with the clients is highly structured.** In psychotherapy the structure, beyond the basic office space, is left largely up to the client. What the client wants to talk about is what shapes the therapist-client time. The PC typically has highly structured time. There will be rules of communication and engagement. Clients may meet in separate rooms. Clients may be assessed fees at a differential rate if they sandbag the proceedings or otherwise cause disruptive uproar. Conflict management is PC driven, not client driven. This shift requires a great deal of relearning for many therapists. In therapy, the belief is that the expression of anger cleanses the system. In PC work, the expression of anger can escalate to the point of incoherence and rigidity. A PC, therefore, is much more active and intrusive to the dynamic between the clients. Again, concrete problem solving rather than "flushing the emotional system" of one or both of the parents is the goal.
- **A PC makes decisions that can be viewed as criticisms by one or both of the clients.** One or both parents will be periodically angry at the PC. Issues must be reframed so that the focus is on the child's needs, not the parents' opinions of each other or their attempts to control each other or the PC. A therapist avoids judging the client because that would harm the therapist–client relationship and probably cause the client to terminate the relationship.

Despite the technical distinctions between PC work and psychotherapy, the high conflict PCs deal with, regardless of their background training, is different from normal conflict. At its most extreme, it may well manifest as conflict without pause that moves with remarkable blindness to destroy another person. To live this aberrant life takes a toll, as does living parallel to it. For a PC, being bathed in anger and rage frequently has an impact. Anger is not "bad" in any absolute sense. Used appropriately, it can be a warning device to others: "Pay attention! Something is wrong and needs to be fixed!" In contrast, anger in high conflict calls attention more to a person's internal reality, not a potentially externally shared reality. Healthy anger alerts and activates constructive problem solving. High-conflict anger batters others again and again with a nonshared reality; its goal is to win, not to problem solve. Such anger is unnerving and draining to its targets, the PC included. One must be able to regenerate and nourish oneself to survive in this aberrant life space.

PCs are routinely castigated, the target of overt anger toward them and the target of anger displaced from a spouse, a parent, a lawyer, or a judge. If one is sensitive to rejection, or intimidated by direct anger, dealing with such clients without slipping into depression, defensiveness, authoritarian arrogance, or a profound sense of incompetence can be a great struggle. One of the greatest challenges for a PC is to see that he or she is doing a good job even though the clients are angry with him or her. Other than professional athletes and the police, this is perhaps the only area of work where one is periodically savaged by people whom society would deem in all other aspects as "normal." One can get very off center with oneself if swept up continuously in the hostile projections of others. One must be constantly vigilant and aware if one is on the slippery slope toward depression, burnout, counteranger, or imperious arrogance. Such reactions are destructive to oneself, the parents, and the children. One must have a strong belief that one's actions are in the best interests of the child, even if they enrage one or both of the adults. One must move one's assessment of self-worth outside of the transaction with the parents to some other source.

Not only do PCs have to deal with the rage of their clients, they must also handle their own anger (at times rage) at the parents. It is impossible not to react with many emotions when one sees the damage that can be wrought on the children by high conflict. PCs experience sadness, helplessness, fear, anxiety, and the weight of responsibility when having to make a decision, at times when no good ones are available. The emotional toll can be very high. PCs often wake in the night worrying about the children affected by their work. There are moments when one feels the sweet satisfaction that something one did has had a positive effect on a family, but unfortunately these moments never seem as frequent as one would like.

Working in this field of endeavor demands that the PC, in addition to having a great sensitivity to his or her own twangs and pings warning of meltdown, also develop a restorative regimen soon after starting PC work. For us, this book was restorative. A peer support group of other PCs can be enormously helpful in keeping oneself in balance. The idea is to keep your head while those about you are losing theirs. We all have our own rejuvenating path. For many it is loving their work. Working with high-conflict couples is perhaps one area where one's work can become part of the problem. Whatever helps you keep perspective is essential to survival and avoiding burnout. A four-year-old client of one of the authors was once asked what he did to make himself feel good when his parents had been fighting. He replied: "I ask for macaroni and cheese and I cuddle with my grandma!" We leave you with this wise idea; just do your own variation.

References

Albee, E. (1988). *Who's Afraid of Virginia Woolf?* New York: New American Library.

Block, J., Block, J. H., and Gjerde, P. J. (1988). Parental functioning and the home environment in families of divorce: prospective and concurrent analyses. *Journal of the American Academy of Child and Adolescent Psychiatry* 27:207–213.

Camara, K. A., and Resnick, G. (1987). Marital and parental subsystems in mother-custody, father-custody and two-parent households: effects on children's social development. In *Advances in Family Assessment, Intervention and Research*, vol. 4, ed. J. Vincent, pp. 165–196. Greenwich, CT: JAI.

Chadman, E. E. (1899). I. Bl. Com., 452; Van Valkenburg v. Watson, 13 Johns., 418. In *Home Law School Series, No. III: Personal Rights and the Domestic Relations.* Conneaut, OH: Home Study Publishing.

Cherlin, A. J., Furstenberg, F. F., Chase-Lansdale, L., et al. (1991). Longitudinal studies of effects of divorce on children in Great Britain and the United States. *Science* 251:1386–1389.

Cowen, E. L., Pedro-Carroll, J. L., and Alpert-Gillis, L. J. (1990). Relationship between support and adjustment among children of divorce. *Journal of Child Psychology and Psychiatry* 31:727–735.

Cowley, C. (1890). *Our Divorce Courts, Their Origin and History: Why They Are Needed, How They Are Abused, and How They May Be Reformed*, 2nd ed. Lowell, MA: Penhallow.

Emery, R. E., and Forehand, R. (1994). Parental divorce and children's well-being: a focus on resilience. In *Stress Risk and Resilience in Children and Adolescents*, ed. R. J. Haggarty et al., pp. 64–99. New York: Cambridge University Press.

Fisher, R., Kopelman, E., and Schneider, A. K. (1994). *Beyond Machiavelli*. Cambridge, MA: Harvard University Press.

Garrity, C., and Baris, M. (1994). *Caught in the Middle: Protecting the Children of High-Conflict Divorce*. San Francisco: Jossey-Bass.

Gelman, D. (1991). The miracle of resiliency. *Newsweek* 117(26): 44–47.

Gold, L. (1992). *Between Love and Hate: A Guide to Civilized Divorce*. New York: Plenum.

Goleman, D. (1995). *Emotional Intelligence: Why It Can Matter More than IQ*. New York: Bantam.

Greenberg, S. A., and Shuman, D. W. (1997). Irreconcilable conflict between therapeutic and forensic roles. *Professional Psychology* 28(1):50–57.

Halem, L. C. (1980). *Divorce Reform*. New York: Free Press.

Hetherington, E. M., Hagan, S., and Anderson, E. R. (1989). Marital transitions: a child's perspective. *The American Psychologist* 44(2):303–312.

Johnston, J., and Campbell, L. E. G. (1988). *Impasses of Divorce: The Dynamics and Resolution of Family Conflict*. New York: Free Press.

Johnston, J., and Roseby, V. (1997). *In the Name of the Child.* New York: Free Press.

Johnston, J., and Straus, R. (1999). Traumatized children in supervised visitation. *Family and Conciliation Court Review* 37(2):135–158.

Katz, M. (1997). *On Playing a Poor Hand Well: Insights from the Lives of Those Who Have Overcome Childhood Risks and Adversities.* New York: W. W. Norton.

Kempton, T., Armistead, L., Wierson, M., and Forehand, R. (1991). Presence of a sibling as a potential buffer following parent divorce: an examination of young adolescents. *Journal of Clinical Child Psychology* 20:434–438.

Kitchen, S. B. (1992). *A History of Divorce.* London: Chapman & Hall.

Kopetski, L. (1991). *Parental alienation syndrome: recent research.* Paper presented at Fifteenth Annual Child Custody Conference, Keystone, CO.

Maccoby, E. E., and Mnookin, R. H. (1992). *Dividing the Child: Social and Legal Dilemmas of Custody.* Cambridge, MA: Harvard University Press.

Mason, M. A. (1994). *From Father's Property to Children's Rights: The History of Child Custody in the United States.* New York: Columbia University Press.

——— (1999). *The Custody Wars.* New York: Basic Books.

Moore, C. (1996). *The Mediation Process, 2nd Edition.* San Francisco: Jossey-Bass.

Rutter, M. (1987). Psychosocial resilience and protective mechanisms. *American Journal of Orthopsychiatry* 57:316–331.

Seligman, Martin E. P. (1996). *The Optimistic Child: A Proven Program to Safeguard Children against Depression and Build Lifelong Resilience.* New York: HarperCollins.

Stolorow, R. D., and Lachman, F. M. (1980). *The Psychoanalysis of Developmental Arrests: Theory and Treatment.* New York: International Universities Press.

Sydlik, B. (1999). *Interventions for High-Conflict Families: A National Perspective.* Salem, OR: Office of the State Court Administrator, Oregon Judicial Department.

Wallerstein, J., and Lewis, J. (1998). The long-term impact of divorce on children. *Family and Conciliation Court Review* 36(3):368–383.

Index

About the Authors

Mitchell Baris, Ph.D., has been a practicing therapist, evaluator, mediator, expert witness, and consultant for the past twenty-five years in the Boulder, Colorado area. Combining his expertise with children and his family therapy skills, he initially worked in the divorce field as a custody evaluator and designed developmentally based parenting plans. With Carla Garrity, he co-authored *Children of Divorce*, a volume that courts have adopted to define developmental standards for parental time sharing in divorce. He has also co-authored *Caught in the Middle* and *Through the Eyes of Children*. Together, Drs. Baris and Garrity have conducted workshops and training in high-conflict mediation and parent coordination in the United States and Canada.

Christine Coates, M.Ed., J.D., is a family law attorney who emphasizes ADR in domestic relations. She was named Outstanding Young Lawyer in Colorado in 1986 by the Colorado Bar Association, and also chosen 1996 Mediator of the Year by the Colorado Council of Mediators and Mediation Organizations. She received the 1999 Community Service Award from the Boulder Interdisciplinary Committee on Child Custody, and is a past president of the Association of Family and Conciliation Courts. A frequent lecturer on family law, professionalism, and dispute resolution options, Ms. Coates is an adjunct professor of domestic relations at the University of Colorado School of Law and of family ADR at the University of Denver.

Betsy Barbour Duvall, M.S.W., a licensed clinical social worker and a board certified diplomate in clinical social work, is a psychotherapist and mediator in private practice in Denver. She was chosen as class speaker at her MSW graduation. She has had formal training in both mediation and mediation-arbitration. Ms. Duvall is a member of the National Association of Social Workers and has been chair of the Colorado chapter's ethics committee, as well as a member of the Board of Directors of the Colorado

Society for Clinical Social Work. She is a frequent speaker on aspects of high-conflict divorce.

Carla Garrity, Ph.D., has been a child psychologist, school consultant, and program developer for the past twenty-five years in the Denver area. In 1978 she formed an interdisciplinary group, The Neuro Developmental Center, for the evaluation and treatment of children, and for many years taught child psychopathology at the School of Professional Psychology at the University of Denver. More recently, she has developed preventative programs for schools and parents in the field of bullying. With Mitchell Baris, Dr. Garrity has authored *Children of Divorce, Caught in the Middle,* and *Through the Eyes of Children,* the latter an anthology of stories offering children coping strategies. Together they have contributed a chapter on divorce mediation to the *Clinical Handbook of Marriage and Couples Intervention.*

Elaine Johnson, J.D., is a trial attorney in Boulder. She is a partner in Johnson and Johnson, P.C., a practice limited to family law. She is past president of the Boulder County Bar Association, past chair of the family law section, and past president of the Boulder Interdisciplinary Committee on Child Custody. The recipient of numerous awards and recognition for her work in the area of domestic relations and for her work with the poor, Ms. Johnson has taught extensively on issues related to family law.

E. Robert LaCrosse, Ph.D., has taught at Harvard, his alma mater, and served as President of Pacific Oaks College in Pasadena, CA. He has been a child clinical psychologist in private practice for the past twenty years in Denver. His practice focuses on divorce issues with children and adults; his interest in high-conflict couples grew from doing custody evaluations with a colleague. Current interests include professional issues confronted when shifting from therapist to conflict manager, the care and nurturance of those who work with people who are in constant conflict and rage, and the psychodynamics of high-conflict couples.